LITERALLY UNBELIEVABLE

Stories from an East Oakland Classroom

Joan -
Thank you for caring
about the kids!

BRONWYN HARRIS

Editor: *Julia Watson*
Copyeditor: *Christine Osborne*
Author Photograph: *Merrilee Willoughby*
Cover Design: *Damian Ludwig*
Book Composition: *Marites D. Bautista*

1 2 3 4 5 6 7 8 9 0
ISBN-13: 978-1535582551
www.bronwynharrisauthor.com

"Why are schools failing vulnerable students? To answer this question, we must start by understanding the challenges facing teachers in an underserved community. In *Literally Unbelievable*, Bronwyn Harris stretches our imaginations, informs our minds, and widens our hearts with an honest and compassionate account of teaching in Oakland. Harris skillfully weaves in true stories to make this book an unforgettable read for anyone who cares about education and children."

—MITALI PERKINS,
Children's book author and lecturer at Saint Mary's College of California

"Bronwyn Harris has done a remarkable job capturing the honest stories of her experiences teaching for eight years in one of the most violent and needy neighborhoods of Oakland. She is descriptive when she could have been castigating. She is even plain at times, letting the tortured facts scream for themselves. She is compassionate while clear thinking. This insider's look is not voyeuristic but seeks to be redemptive by telling the truth and letting those of us not inside see and feel and understand so much more than we would otherwise be able to do. The question it begs is: what can and should be done?"

—REV. MARK LABBERTON, Ph.D.,
President, Fuller Theological Seminary

"Bronwyn is a gifted storyteller who takes us on a journey of real pain, beauty, and hope inside the East Oakland classroom. As she says, education is about more than a curriculum, more than surviving, but rather about creating safe spaces for children to learn, grow, and thrive. Together we are called to stir the dreams and hopes of 'our kids.'"

—REV. DR. MARY GLENN,
Fuller Youth Institute Faculty, City Net Co-Director

"This book takes me right back to my days working down the street from Ms. Harris. Her stories of our kids and our classrooms bring back vivid memories of the love, exhaustion, sadness, and so many more emotions that I felt. This book offers an accessible, sobering introduction to under-resourced public schools for those wishing to learn 'what it's really like.' But it also conveys the profound richness and importance of the students that this system has left behind. This should be required reading for all prospective teachers, policy makers, and researchers."

—EMILY PENNER, Ph.D.,
Assistant Professor of Education, UC Irvine

"I knew 'East Oakland Elementary' was one of the more challenging, under-resourced schools surrounded by a plethora of poverty and violence. I knew there had been a revolving door of principals, but didn't know that during your eight years of teaching (at EOE) eight principals entered and exited. That in itself is cause for alarm and symptomatic of a broken education system. I too have seen firsthand the disparities in many of our Oakland schools. But I remind myself and others that if we only wring our hands we can't use them to reach out. Children are precious, human beings, created in the image of God. Children are our future. As Harris says, '*Our* kids. Every one of them is worth fighting for. My greatest hope is that more people will see this and, like I have, will make it their own fight.'"

—RANDY ROTH,
President, Faith Network of the East Bay, Inc.

For my beloved former students:
I am so proud of all of you. You weren't given easy lives,
but you've persevered. Thank you for everything you've taught me.

For Akilah, my "Little Sister":
I have no doubt that you will make an impact on the world.

For Carlos: I have all faith.

For FD, JH, and JG-L: We lost you too soon.

CONTENTS

MY DREAM

Dr. Martin Luther King Jr. had a dream that there would be equality and peace. Dr. King wanted his children not to be judged by the color of their skin but by the content of their character.

I have a dream that when I grow up I can go to college and work very hard so I could get a great job, and live a long, happy and harmless life. I hope and pray that I won't get killed or die early.

I have a dream that none of my family will be killed or die unnaturally. I also want my little brothers to grow up and be whatever they want to be.

I have a dream that my community won't have any more shootings, especially people in my family. Specifically, my cousin. At sixteen, shot and killed, who I love so much.

I have a dream that this country will never again have segregation, discrimination, and people being treated badly because of the color of their skin. (Like Dr. King said.)

I have a dream that the world would be a better place. I think that Dr. Martin Luther King Jr. would love this nation today because his dreams came true. There is equality and peace in the world today. His children aren't solely being judged by the color of their skin, but by the content of their character.

—Akilah, fourth grade student in Oakland, CA

INTRODUCTION

For eight years, I taught at an elementary school in the most violent neighborhood of Oakland, California. Most years, the majority of the students in my class personally knew someone who had been murdered. All of them knew of someone who had been killed—either accidentally (usually by a stray bullet) or intentionally. Far too many of them had actually witnessed a shooting.

This placement was my first job as a new teacher. I was twenty-four years old and had been trained in how to set up a classroom, how to assess reading levels, and how to do read-alouds of Caldecott Award–winning picture books. However, I was not remotely prepared to deal with children who had seen unimaginable violence, to teach an incomplete curriculum, to help students whose parents showed up to school drunk or high, or to handle incompetent or destructive administrators. I watched my coworkers leave one after the other until, at age thirty-one, I was the senior teacher at my school.

Today, it's been over nine years since I left the classroom and I miss it. I miss being surrounded by beautiful, funny, intelligent students who are just starting to think critically. I miss their amazingly descriptive writing.

I loved when former students came to my classroom to visit, especially all the way from their middle or high schools. I miss the incredible relationships that I developed with my students' families, regardless of our socioeconomic and racial differences (but only after they really, really understood that I loved their children).

I miss it, but at the same time, I am also relieved not to be teaching anymore. I'm no longer tired all the time. I don't have my heart broken on a daily basis by what the kids have had to endure. I'm not spending money I don't have on school supplies.

I'll never forget my teaching experience. Some things in particular stick with me. For instance, I can't forget the many times I had to call Child Protective Services, and why. Or kids putting their heads down and saying, "You can't help me. Nobody can help me. I should just die." I'll remember the notes asking for homework to be excused because of gunfire just outside of a student's home the previous night.

It broke my heart when kids asked me why their dad didn't love them, or why drugs made their mom forget she had a family. I cried after a field trip where I saw the meanest, dirtiest, rudest kid in my third grade class care for a rat with all the tenderness that child himself deserved, but had never received.

Leaving the classroom was one of the hardest decisions I have ever made, and I still question it sometimes. I miss the job and I miss the children, but I couldn't keep working under the conditions I faced.

It was simply not sustainable—not without the real and lasting changes needed to fix a broken educational system that is failing so many of our most vulnerable kids.

My Story

When I was teaching in Oakland, I stuck out. There was just no way around it. The most obvious difference was my race, as there were literally no Caucasians living in the African American, Latino, and Asian neighborhood where I was teaching. I soon learned that my socioeconomic class was an even bigger difference—although at first, this wasn't as obvious to me.

Growing up, my family was by no means wealthy—we all worked our way through college and I don't think any of us has ever owned a new car. But we also never had to deal with poverty or extreme violence where we lived. We never experienced hunger, eviction, trying to buy groceries without a car, or the violent death of a friend or family member—all normal parts of life for my students.

When I first started working at East Oakland Elementary School, I didn't know much about the neighborhood. I had heard about the "bad" parts of Oakland and seen them in the news, but I quickly learned that much of the violence happening there was so routine that it was taken for granted and didn't even receive news coverage.

Most of the incidents not considered newsworthy were homicides, but there were other violent assaults that went largely ignored by local media as well. One that actually made the news involved the mother of one of my students being pushed out of a moving car by her boyfriend while they were both high. She got caught in the seatbelt and dragged for several blocks, losing 50 percent of the skin on her body.

Her son came back to school soon after the incident, but there was no one available on-campus trained to help our students cope with trauma, since we had no school counselor that year. He was one of many students who needed the kinds of services that were available when and where I went to school as a child—services now routinely slashed from school budgets as "nonessential."

Given my initial shock at the conditions when I arrived at the school, I was able to adapt to teaching in the neighborhood fairly quickly. My secret was becoming immediately invested in the lives of my students and their families. Building relationships with them was incredibly rewarding in ways I hadn't expected.

At first, I was an outsider. But over time, I became a trusted member of this community. In some cases, I was the first white person that my students' parents had ever trusted. I learned volumes about other cultures, and in the process, about myself. Together, we made great strides in academic and emotional learning. We celebrated and mourned together. I am forever changed by having loved this community's children.

However, the poor working conditions at the school and the resulting stress inevitably took a serious toll on me. I tried to stick it out for the kids' sakes, and I outlasted many of my colleagues. But in the end, there was a price to pay for staying as long as I did. My health and my personal life suffered, and I ended up resigning in discouragement, feeling burned out and cynical.

It was only after my body, my mind, my heart, and my spirit had time to heal that I regained a sense of hope—not only for myself, but for the kids whose lives I was a part of for so many years.

Why I Wrote This Book

Now that I am no longer in the classroom, I often feel less able to help my former students. I've kept in touch with many of them, and I'm also a Big Sister through Big Brothers Big Sisters, which is particularly rewarding, but it's not the same as being in the classroom.

I know I couldn't save my former students from the struggles they faced every day even if I were still their teacher. I remember how exhausted I was for eight years and how very sick I became at the end. But there are kids who need help, and it hurts my heart that I can't do more.

There's a familiar, sappy story about a little boy who goes walking along the shore after a big storm and sees thousands of starfish washed up on the beach. He starts picking them up and flinging them back into the ocean, when a cynical adult comes along and says, "There are thousands of starfish. You'll never make a difference." The kid responds, "But I've made a difference to this starfish."

It's sweet, heartwarming, and inspiring. But there are so many starfish left. And kids aren't starfish. With enough failures at school and at home, with enough adults telling them they're bad or a disappointment, kids learn to believe that they are unlovable, unworthy, and have no chance of success. They learn to hate themselves more than anyone else could ever hate them.

That's why I started writing about these kids—first as a blog I kept for seven years while teaching. Initially, I wrote for myself in journal-style entries, as a creative outlet for work-related stress. But in making the blog public, I found that I was raising awareness. Other people could now see the incredible struggles that my students faced on a daily basis.

I was often shocked at what these children had experienced or witnessed, but my friends found it so hard to believe these stories that many of them simply couldn't. One friend explained to me, "We know you aren't lying, but this stuff . . . it's literally unbelievable."

Literally unbelievable, but all too true.

Kids who grow up in impoverished neighborhoods like the one I taught in deal with hunger, homelessness, gun violence, neglect, and abuse every day. What's more, the schools in these neighborhoods lack the funds and other resources (e.g., school nurses, counselors, etc.) required to give kids who need it the most the help, support, and skills needed to cope with the difficulties they face. The system is stacked against them.

Change is needed, and it will only come if enough people see the heartbreaking conditions these kids are growing up in—not in a developing country halfway around the world, but right here in the United States.

My hope is that maybe if people see how many starfish are still washed up on the shore, they'll help throw them back. Maybe people will see each of these kids as a person and think about how that teenager they think of as a "thug," who looks scary to them in his hoodie and sagging pants, was once a little boy—maybe even a little boy who once asked me why his dad didn't love him.

If enough people can see that and are motivated to help, maybe it will make a small difference—or a big difference—to even just one kid who needs help.

Education is about more than a curriculum. It is also about a learning environment; some learning environments enable children to thrive, while others work against even the most promising, motivated students.

We as educators, concerned parents, and citizens may not be able to change the greater environment, but we can affect the learning environment of our schools. If we wouldn't expect middle class white kids to learn in these conditions, why do we accept and expect it for other communities' children?

This book is my way of pointing out how many starfish are on the beach, right here in our own backyard.

Here are their stories. When I quote students, I have kept their natural speech patterns, which are sometimes different than my own. I have changed the names (of both people and places, including the name of the school) to protect the privacy of those I've written about. I offer their stories to you in the hope that, together, we can find real-world solutions to the inequity that plagues the education and daily lives of children all over America.

Not "those kids." *Our* kids.

Every one of them is worth fighting for. My greatest hope is that more people will see this and, as I have, make it their own fight.

CHAPTER 1:

SCRAMBLING FOR CLASSROOM RESOURCES

"No matter what happens in a child's home, no matter what other social and economic factors may impede a child, there's no question in my mind that a first-rate school can transform almost everything."
—JONATHAN KOZOL

Transforming a Broken Learning Environment

The school where I taught was a dirty, bare-looking place, and had been that way for a long time. It was a magnet for graffiti, and for much of one school year, the portable classroom in which I taught third grade had the word "rape" scrawled on the outside wall in large letters. Throughout my time there—and afterward—things gradually improved. At one point, newly planted trees made a big difference, even if they were a little scrawny. A friend painted vibrant murals, which also helped brighten up the campus.

The year after I stopped teaching at East Oakland Elementary, I came back to visit, to volunteer in the classroom and catch up with my former students and colleagues.

That first day back as a volunteer, I walked into the cafeteria to find it totally transformed. With a teacher's help, the kids had turned it into a temporary art installation, and the whole feeling of the place was different. The students were enthralled and looked around in wonder. Children avoided fighting because they were so proud of their work and so enamored of the patchwork quilt of student art completely covering every wall.

It was beautiful—both the art and the human reactions.

The school still had plenty of problems: racial tensions, graffiti on the mural in the front of the school, extreme violence in the neighborhood, and more. But this display of artwork provided hope, along with a lightness and playfulness that had been missing when I was teaching there.

Environment truly makes a difference in learning and in creating community. These changes to the school's environment didn't always go smoothly, however. One year our playground was remodeled. It was shiny, new, and exciting. The best part was a big play structure with monkey bars, slides, ladders, poles to slide down, and all sorts of fun things. It was fantastic.

But a year later, the slightly spongy squishy material under the structure started coming apart. The entire play structure was deemed unsafe and was slated to be fixed "right away." Many months later, it was finally "fixed" and the kids got to play on it again . . . for two days. Then it was labeled unsafe again. None of us at the school could detect any visible difference between the play structure's "safe" and "unsafe" states.

For my final two years of teaching, the kids had to look at this wonderful play structure without being allowed to touch it. It was like torture for them, being tantalized with the hope of fun that they couldn't experience. Every couple of weeks, a voice over the loudspeaker reminded them they needed to stay off the play structure. When they succumbed and played on it anyway, they were disciplined.

Is there any child who can resist the temptation of getting on a play structure when someone's not looking? The playground was an example of the "looks good on paper" but starkly different reality of the resources that were being provided to the students across the board.

Problem #1: Lack of Resources

For those of us who love teaching, it is an incredibly rewarding profession—except, of course, monetarily. Low teacher salaries are something our society just seems to take for granted, like potholes or the inability of Congress to pass gun control. And yet, despite how little we're paid, teachers end up spending a big chunk of their paycheck on professional expenses.

At the beginning of each school year, I spent hundreds of dollars on much-needed supplies. The school provided a few basics, but it stands to reason that children might use more than four pencils and one box of crayons over the course of the entire school year. (That's not a typo—four pencils were allotted per year for an eight-year-old student.) So, like other teachers, I bit the bullet and bought those "extra" supplies myself.

During any given year, I bought crayons, watercolors, markers, chalk, dry erase markers, colored pencils, notebooks, erasers, rulers, folders, scissors, and glue for all twenty or so of my students. I also had to buy electric pencil sharpeners, because the wall-mounted sharpener in our room never worked, ever. Many of the books that I used to create homework packets were mine, as were the posters, stickers, soap, paper towels, and cleaning spray.

Oh, and the printer. And the stool that I sat on at the front of the classroom. Sure, the district provided the textbooks, but basically all of the literature in the classroom, and all the videos and games were mine, not to mention the kickballs, footballs, and jump ropes, all of which had a distressing tendency to break, pop, or accidentally get tossed on the roof. Playground equipment frequently had to be replaced.

That said, I was fortunate. I had more class donations than anyone else who worked at the school. I didn't have to buy the fans (the temperature in my classroom got as high as 95 degrees in the spring), the computers, the laminator, the plants, or the reading chairs, because they were all donated. Through the educational charity DonorsChoose, I obtained an abacus for each student, as well as hand sanitizer, Kleenex, class pets, flashcards (though I bought a ton of those myself, too), timers, and spelling dictionaries.

I don't want to sound ungrateful. Over time, the school provided more supplies. I had friends, family, and total strangers who generously attended to the things my students needed to learn. But at times, it just felt like too much to do to arrange all the donations, and the cost of the supplies I was buying was a significant burden on a teacher's meager salary.

Reams of Help

The most generous donation of school supplies came in my second year of teaching, in a rather spectacular manner. Just two years in, I was already exhausted. I was trying to learn how to teach third grade and prepare the kids for standardized tests, all the while dealing with an administrator whose favorite line was "I can have your job, you know!"

When the curriculum required the kids to cut and paste, I put in my request for scissors and glue. But the person in charge of supplies rolled her eyes and said, "We don't have *those*." Her manner clearly suggested I was clueless as to how schools worked, and in that moment, something in me snapped.

This was the beginning of my begging the people I knew for help.

After quickly exhausting the resources of teacher friends who had extra supplies (yes, this was back in the day when some schools actually had extra supplies and my friends may have let me "borrow" some), I turned to Craigslist. I put up a post on the "items wanted" section saying that I was teaching at an under-resourced school and that we desperately needed supplies, listing which items would be helpful. I got a handful of people who had a few pair of scissors or some scratch paper, or just good hearts and encouragement. I also received two emails that stood out.

One was from a remarkably angry person who never used his or her name, but who stated—using an awful lot of exclamation marks—that privileged do-gooder teachers needed to come to the realization that there is no amount of glue or scissors in the world that can help these children in their education, and that simply providing them with glue and scissors instead of a quality education was only hurting them and who did I think I was anyway?

The other was more helpful. It was from a man named Karl who wanted to know if I would like some paper. Of course I wanted paper. He said he had a lot and that he'd bring it in his pickup, if that was okay.

And boy—did that man have *paper*.

Karl drove up in a big, beat-up old pickup truck. He was a big guy in late middle-age wearing overalls. His explanation for the paper was that he owned a storage facility and someone had left all this paper in one of the units. He wanted it to go to good use.

The truck bed was overflowing with boxes and boxes of paper—enough that it took up half the space in my garage after we unloaded all of it.

It came in different colors and sizes, too—white, salmon, and light blue, 11 x 17, 11 x 14, and standard printer-size. Once we got it all unloaded, I couldn't stop staring, because there was simply *so much* of it. The salmon and blue paper was faded, but all the white paper was in good shape. There were also a few boxes of thick, high-quality light blue paper—almost cardstock—that was glossy on one side.

That week I loaded up as many boxes as would fit in my car and brought them to school. I put a sign out for the other teachers saying that I had a lot of paper and to please take some. People would come by, thinking I'd give them half a ream, and I'd give them seven or eight reams. They kept asking if it was really okay for them to take it, because we were all used to hoarding supplies. I kept bringing more paper from home until everyone had enough.

The problem was that I still had a garage full of paper. Handing it out to the almost forty teachers at my school hadn't really made a dent in it. I brought as much to school as would fit in my classroom and stacked paper in every empty space, on every bookshelf, and in all the filing cabinets. I never used the copy machine paper anymore because we were always running out of it in the supply room. I just brought my own. The kids liked having worksheets and homework on light blue and salmon-colored paper. They loved the glossy blue paper and used it for painting, drawing, and home art projects.

For the next *six years,* whenever we had standardized tests, an administrator would come to me and ask if I still had some of that extra paper and I'd supply the whole school with scratch paper for the math section. I gave stacks of it to kids who liked to draw, first in my class, and then, as word spread, to kids all over the school who came looking for it. I gave it away on Freecycle to other teachers at other schools. I moved boxes of it from one classroom to another and from one house to another.

That paper was like the loaves and the fishes and the Hanukkah oil all in one. It just didn't run out.

When I finished teaching, I still had a stack of blue paper that was probably equal to five or six reams. I continued to use it as printer paper and then scratch printer paper, when one side was used.

Not long ago, I used the very last piece—over a decade after Karl brought that truckload to my house. I have an editing project printed on the blue paper, and now that I've finished the project, it's time to get rid of the printed version.

It's a little silly, but there's a part of me that wanted to keep that one last piece of blue paper.

It Takes a Village

Cleaning up the campus and securing enough school supplies weren't the only kinds of help I needed to teach effectively in the challenging learning environment my students and I shared. Visitors and volunteers helped show my kids more of the world outside East Oakland and gave them a tangible human presence outside the classroom.

We were blessed with volunteers who showed up to help and teach the kids, and who showed interest in and concern for them. The more of these adults they interacted with, the better the kids did in general.

Truly, I had some of the most overqualified volunteers ever in my third grade class. This may have had something to do with the fact that I shamelessly begged my friends to help in any way possible. I think there were a few new friends who I asked to come as soon as I met them, before I was entirely sure of their names. Some of these volunteers included:

- Reading tutors with an MFA or a graduate degree in physical therapy.
- PhD candidates in engineering from Stanford and UC Berkeley who helped the kids with math.
- My extremely talented and musical brother, who brought in his drums several times.
- PhD candidates in engineering from UC Berkeley, who taught the kids about construction (several years in a row) and helped with a field trip.
- A friend from Pixar, who got us tours three different years. And once, when they were no longer giving tours, who came to my classroom to sign the kids' toys from *Cars*.
- Athletes from UC Berkeley who helped with not just physical education, but a whole variety of subjects.
- A special education teacher who organized my whole classroom for me.

There were many more volunteers. I can't list them all, but I am so grateful to everyone who came in and shared their time, skills, and talents with my students. The volunteers who came to help the kids learn new things really made a lasting impression on them—and none more so than Carol.

At the time, Carol ran the children's ministries department at my church and offered to come and volunteer at my school. She had volunteered in a kindergarten class the year before.

She started by reading with the kids and helping them with their practice tests. As she got to know them, she saw that many of the kids had a creative side all but bursting to come out. Since we had limited resources at the school, she brought in supplies for art projects. And these were *fun* projects: painting wood shapes, making journals using cut-outs from animal magazines and foam stickers, clay projects, Easter baskets with silk flowers and other decorations, St. Patrick's Day projects, and all sorts of exciting crafts.

The kids loved it because they got to be creative in new ways and didn't have to ration supplies, since Carol always brought more than enough.

Then the snacks started coming. I forget what the first snack was that Carol brought, but I remember that the kids loved it and ate all the extras. Many of my students faced hunger on a regular basis. Carol saw that the kids were hungry and, after that, she brought them all sorts of food that was healthier than most of the snacks they were used to: granola bars, fruit bars, apples, grilled cheese sandwiches, hot dogs, milk, and bottles of water. They loved those; I think they felt like adults with their bottled water.

The way the kids responded to Carol showed that they appreciated the love and care behind the gifts she gave them—not just the crafts and food. They would ask me every week when Carol was coming back, and they'd get excited on the days she was actually scheduled to be there. They would have loved doing arts and crafts with anyone, but getting to do fun activities with someone who lavished such care upon them was special.

Even the food and drinks she brought them tasted better to them than other food. One student, Nancy, wondered if the cafeteria milk was expired (it wasn't). Why else would it not taste as good as the milk that Carol brought for snack? Her classmate, Ray, answered her, saying, "The milk Carol brings us tastes better because Carol loves us."

It never escaped these kids' notice when people truly cared about them. And the more love and fun I was able to beg, plead, and cajole into the classroom for them, the more our learning environment was enriched. I can't overstate what a huge difference this made—not just in their excitement for learning, but for so many of them, in their sense of self-worth and what was possible in their lives.

I sometimes worried that the kids would feel like charity cases, receiving free food, books, and school supplies, along with all of the free volunteer help. I was totally wrong. They saw this as an expression of people caring about them. One of them even said to me, "All these people give us things because they think we're so special!" I'm sure there are situations in which it is humiliating to accept free food or other assistance, and I don't want to diminish those feelings. But over and over, I saw my students thrive from all the help we got, and we were extremely fortunate that our volunteers and donors came in with open hearts and minds to actually make a difference.

CHAPTER 2:

A SAFE PLACE TO LEARN

"*But you know, there are no children here. They've seen too much to be children.*"

—ALEX KOTLOWITZ,
There Are No Children Here

Shots in the Night

In my second year of teaching, I got a note that read, "Please excuse my daughter from not doing her homework. The gangs was shooting and she had to sleep in the closet." Other kids would talk about sleeping in the bathtub in case bullets from drive-by shootings went through walls, reasoning that they probably wouldn't go through the bathtub too. I was so shocked that I didn't even know how to respond.

What was shocking to me was common reality to them. Not just once in their lifetimes, but many, many nights, my students heard shooting and were afraid for their lives. Some were even so used to the sound of gunfire in their neighborhoods that they could *sleep right through it*. I'm not sure which is worse—that there are kids who stay up at night, afraid of being killed in their sleep, or that others are so inured to such extreme violence that they can sleep through gunfire.

This is not in an official war zone, or in the Third World, but less than four miles from some of the most affluent neighborhoods in the Bay Area.

My family and my friends don't have to worry about stray bullets because we have enough money to live in a safe area. My students didn't.

We are the world's most prosperous, powerful nation, and yet we have children in our midst who are completely used to the danger of being *accidentally shot in their sleep*.

When the Virginia Tech shooting happened in 2007, it was revealing—and disheartening—to hear what the kids had to say. None of them seemed shocked. Instead, their reaction was deep empathy and sadness.

One little girl told me she had seen the Virginia Tech shooting on the news. She added that her neighbors (other kids at the school) had almost gotten caught in a shooting the night before that injured another student's cousin. As she related these details to me, my student—just a little girl— had the exhausted, world-weary look of someone used to these kinds of things. Even the way she delivered it—all in one run-on sentence as if she wanted to get it over with and move on—carried an air of resignation. The Virginia Tech shooting was awful. *Awful.* My heart goes out to the families and friends of the victims of that incident and all the others that have taken place since. But I'm also horrified and shocked by the violence my young students saw every day.

None of my teacher training had prepared me for this. I was no more ready for dealing with this kind of trauma than I would have been to treat gaping head wounds or broken bones on the playground. We had a part-time school nurse who could let children lie down and send them home if they threw up but didn't have training in emotional trauma. A school psychologist was assigned to our school for three hours a week, and all of that time was spent testing students for learning disabilities. We had no other counselor except for, one year, a part-time intern who seemed just as overwhelmed as the rest of us.

It's hard to estimate how many of my students could have been diagnosed with post-traumatic stress disorder (PTSD), but I think the number would have been staggering. Research from the ChildTrauma Academy[1] has shown that when a child experiences fear or insecurity, they are not able to learn in the same way as a child who is not traumatized. I was dealing with entire classes suffering from trauma.

At times, the violence that the children experienced in their home lives would bleed into the classroom. The reading curriculum emphasized asking kids to "make connections" between literature and their own lives—finding bits of stories that were familiar in some way, or characters that were like people they knew. That particular day, one of my third graders, Deandre, found a connection to a funny story about a cowboy hiding because he had been threatened by people trying to collect on a small debt. "This is just like what happened to my uncle," he said. "Except they really did kill my uncle when he owed money."

What do you say to that?

His uncle had recently been shot—in broad daylight—near his house, less than a mile from our school. As Deandre had said, his uncle had owed someone money. His was the thirty-third homicide that year in

---

[1] The ChildTrauma Academy (http://www.childtrauma.org) was founded by Dr. Bruce Perry. He summarizes his recommendations for teachers and caregivers in the article "Principles of Working with Traumatized Children" on the Scholastic website: http://teacher.scholastic.com/professional/bruceperry/working_children.htm

Oakland, when the prior year at the same time, there were fourteen. We were on a record-breaking pace.

Keep in mind that Oakland isn't a very big city, with just over 400,000 people; thirty-three homicides is a lot, and that wasn't even the full year's worth. In 2014, Oakland had a murder rate of 19.5 per 100,000 residents, high enough to put it at number 11 for US cities of more than 250,000 people.[2]

Not even six months later, the same student lost another family member—not a blood relative, but someone who was definitely considered family. It was a woman who worked at the daycare run by the kids' great-aunt. They called her their "god-mama." She was hit and killed by a drunk driver.

The middle child in the family, Marcel, came and told me about it. "Too many people been died," he said. Damn right.

The Far-Reaching Effects of Violence on School Communities

Sometimes it wasn't merely echoes of the violence in the home or neighborhood that made it into the classroom. At times, the threat of violence made it into the sanctuary of the school itself.

I was reminded how this reality impacted my students two years after I stopped teaching, when I went to see the fifth grade promotion ceremony for my last set of third grade students.

Fifth graders are adorably funny when it comes to public speaking. As part of the ceremony, one of my former students gave a short speech about going to middle school. She was nervous enough that most of her speech came out like this:

"And-now-that-we-are-being-promoted-from-fifth-grade-we-are-going-to-middle-school-and-we-will-have-to-act-like-little-adults-without-the-kind-of-help-we-are-used-to-from-our-teachers-here-in-elementary-school-when-they-help-us-all-the-time."

What the next speaker shared, though, nearly had me in tears. Her topic was elementary school memories, and she listed ways that she and

---

[2] https://en.wikipedia.org/wiki/List_of_United_States_cities_by_crime_rate_(2014)

other students could tell that their teachers cared about them. Along with "teaching us" and "helping us when we don't know something," she added something unexpected for an elementary school promotion speech. She said, "And our teachers don't let us go to the bathrooms or in the hall when there's shooting."

I knew all too well what she was talking about. At least once a year, our school had a *lockdown*, a physical safety threat where the teachers must lock their classroom doors, close the curtains, turn off the lights, and get the kids in the center of the room if possible.

I didn't always know the reason for the lockdown as it was unfolding. After the fact, we'd learn what the threat had been. Over the years, a few notable lockdowns were called because of a parent running through the school with a gun (a custody battle gone badly), a high-speed chase involving a bank robber over the Bay Bridge that ended in front of our school, and an arson/attempted murder-suicide at a carburetor shop a block down the road.

Most of these events did not even make the local news, so only those from the neighborhood knew they were happening, and the rest of us were kept in the dark about the threat of violence in and around the public elementary school.

Lockdowns entailed a number of problems. First of all, communicating to the staff that a lockdown was underway was a challenge in its own right. Since we changed principals so often, there was never an accepted procedure for any emergency action. Fire drills were pretty much the same from one school to the next, but we never mastered earthquake drills or lockdowns. Sometimes lockdowns were signaled by a series of bells or announced over the loudspeaker, and sometimes the current principal would use some kind of cute code to avoid scaring the children. "Mr. Keys is in the building" was one.

Then there were the logistical problems. At our school, the classroom doors could only be locked from the outside, with a key. That meant that each teacher had to open the door and go out into the hall to lock it—less than ideal if you've just been informed there's a man with a gun running through said hall. I solved this problem by simply keeping my door locked all of the time and making everyone knock to get in. The principals never liked this, but after the first lockdown, I did it anyway.

The next problem was managing a bunch of panicked children who had no idea what was going on and all needed to do two things immediately: call their moms and go to the bathroom. For the emotional need, I would pass around my cell phone in the dark during lockouts. I knew you were supposed to stay silent during a lockdown, but the kids would become hysterical if they didn't know whether or not their family was involved, and that was much louder than a phone call. For the biological need, during long lockdowns, I resorted to letting kids use the sink a couple of times. I had a blanket that someone would hold up, and I cleaned the sink really well after.

One year, in the middle of a lockdown, a student was crying because he was afraid of the man in the hall with a gun—a reasonable enough reaction. Another student said, "But you don't have to worry, because our teacher will never let the man with the gun get to us."

His assurance wasn't because he couldn't fathom the risk; this kid had known plenty of people who were shot and some who were killed. And it wasn't because I was showing bravado either; I wasn't. The other kids agreed, and I knew it was true too—the man with the gun would have had to get to the kids literally over my dead body. It was less of a choice than a fact.

I don't know how else to explain it, but somehow I think that God made sure that if I did nothing else right in all my years of teaching, I was able to make those kids feel safe and rest assured that I would do anything in my power to keep them that way.

That's the same thing that made me want to cry during this little girl's speech at her fifth grade promotion ceremony—the sincerity with which she said she knew her teachers had kept her safe. Just like another kid might say they knew their teacher loved them because she took them on field trips, this one knew her teacher loved her because she wasn't allowed in the hall when there was shooting.

Stop and think about that for a minute. In neighborhoods like this one, violence is such an accepted part of life that a fifth grader used her graduation speech to thank her teachers for protecting her from being shot.

Even more telling: none of the parents batted an eye at the girl's speech. I can just imagine if someone had given that speech at my own childhood elementary school! There would have been an uproar from the assembled parents and families. But not here. No, these parents just nodded, because they too knew that this was one way the teachers took care of their kids.

To Protect and Serve?

While the parents in the neighborhood acknowledged a trusted teacher's role in keeping their kids safe, their relationship with the police was more perilous, which impacted the kids as well.

I was raised to believe that the police were there to help me. I was taught both at school and at home that police officers were safe, helpful people. I learned that their job was to patrol the neighborhood and make it a better place, and that I could always ask any police officer for help if I needed it.

My students had a very different experience.

Many of them had parents who had been mistakenly arrested because they fit the (often very broad) description of a criminal. Others had parents who were arrested with good cause, but were treated much differently than a white suspect in the suburbs might have been. During routine traffic stops, black men I know were thrown up against their car and held at gunpoint, or made to lie on the side of the freeway. Their offense might have been running a red light or having expired registration tags; both things that I have done, but I was treated extremely politely by the police officers who pulled me over. Other children had witnessed their parents calling the police for help, only to find that the police were "too busy" to respond or even appeared uninterested in what was happening.

Before my first lockdown, I asked a student what his family did after a shooting in his neighborhood and if his mom had called the police. He just stared at me and asked blankly, "What they gonna do?" At the time, I didn't realize that I was being naïve about this. Later, when I called to report some middle school students setting fires on our campus and both the police and fire departments told me to deal with it myself, I began to understand the community's frustration.

During one particular lockdown, we tried to get the help of the local police force. A disgruntled father in the middle of a custody dispute had threatened to bring a gun to school and start shooting if he didn't get custody of his child. When we called the authorities, they told us that they wouldn't send an officer unless we knew the first and last name of the father, which—shockingly—he had neglected to give us when phoning in his threat. I mentioned something to the custodian about how outrageous that was and she just looked at me and said flatly, "They don't care. To them, we'd just be one more dead n-----."

The resignation in her voice showed me how tired this community was of not being able to depend on the authorities. I had never thought about it in those terms before—how incredibly draining it would be when you feel that the lives of the people in your community don't matter to the people sworn to serve and protect them.

Another time, there was an attempted kidnapping at our school. A seemingly mentally ill homeless man came in and grabbed one of our fifth grade boys by the jacket and tried to pull him off campus. Fortunately, the boy had enough presence of mind to wriggle out of his jacket and run free. Several staff members called 911, and others called the police department's emergency number.

The police took fifty-five minutes to show up. One of the kids asked me straight out, "Would they have come faster if we was all white kids?" I was so caught off guard that I stuttered and didn't answer directly. Still, I think my fumbling attempt to find words to reassure them was all the answer they needed.

Building a Bridge of Trust

My intent is not to disparage the police in Oakland. They have an extremely difficult job and a complicated relationship with the community, which itself is not entirely blameless. I came away from these experiences with a sense of frustration with the police, and I also developed a deep compassion for the community.

Faultless or not, many people in the neighborhood felt completely unprotected and ignored—like they weren't even worth the basic protection afforded to others. The sense of betrayal was visible in the children, in their parents, and even in the school staff who lived in the community.

As discouraging as this was, it gave me an extremely valuable insight into the heart of the community and a glimpse of why so many of the families in the area didn't trust appointed authority figures, be they teachers, police officers, or social workers. In many ways, this realization was a turning point for me.

When I first came in, I was full of an idealistic desire to help my students. It was only once I tempered my discouragement with a realistic understanding of what the kids and the greater community were up against that I began to be more effective in my teaching duties.

Steps must be taken to repair the broken relationship between the authorities and the people in communities of color. Both parties have to be willing to have the hard conversations required to get to know each other and understand the other party's background. But as one parent told me, once you have had a bad experience with the police, it's hard to imagine calling on them for help.

I think most police officers start out with good intentions of wanting to help people, but grow jaded and fearful after dealing with so many desperate people and dangerous situations. In my experience, this kind of emotional burnout is common among well-intentioned teachers, too.

This lesson for teachers who hope to succeed in inner-city schools is clear but challenging nonetheless: you don't start with the trust of the students or the community. That trust has to be earned. And those past negative interactions that students have had with police, school administrators, and other teachers all color their expectations of how you, the new authority figure, will treat them.

The earlier that this broken relationship with authority can be repaired—one step and one person at a time—the more successful a teacher and his or her students will be. Those building blocks of trust spread to families, and over time, can encompass the community as a whole.

CHAPTER 3:

A BROKEN SYSTEM

"*New teacher support is canceled. I repeat, new teacher support is canceled.*"

—ANNOUNCEMENT OVER THE INTERCOM
   at East Oakland Elementary

The Leadership Vacuum

As if it weren't enough to have students with extremely varying needs, some years I felt as if I had more principals than students. During my eight years at East Oakland Elementary, we went through not one, not two, not even three or four, but *eight* principals. If that's not a symptom of a broken school, I don't know what is.

Turnover was high for teachers as well at East Oakland Elementary, which wasn't difficult to understand. The neighborhood was a notoriously violent area, so it was hard to recruit teachers to work there, and harder still to convince them to stay. As a result, principals had to constantly deal with the necessity of bringing new and often inexperienced teachers on board.

The same intense stress that drove teachers away affected principals. The revolving door of principals, however, had serious ramifications for teachers and students alike. Programs and policies changed drastically with each new administrator. Children often couldn't even remember who the current principal was, sometimes going through three or four names before giving up the effort to recall the current one.

The net result was a nightmarish game of musical bosses with some unique personalities.

Principal Zero

I call him Principal Zero because he left the week before I started teaching. So although I never taught under him, he set the atmosphere at the school when I started. It's clear that he was well respected, though not universally liked. From the descriptions I heard, he was highly effective, rather like an intelligent, soft-spoken drill sergeant. But he left mid-year to take the reins of the middle school next door, which needed a strong hand.

Principal One

Principal One hired me and was my boss for the first eighteen months. Scatterbrained and fond of yelling, she had been the assistant principal under Principal Zero (and previously, a fourth-grade teacher).

I'm told that she was great as an assistant principal, when discipline was her sole focus. Charged with running the entire school, however, she was overwhelmed. She became forgetful and was clearly unhappy in the job—and began to take her frustrations out on the people around her.

For starters, she never got my name right, and mine wasn't the only one. In fact, she usually referred to *all* the teachers—even those she had known for several years—as "Mr. Man" or "Mrs. Lady." Worse, she had a tendency to hold very long staff meetings, in which she would listen to all the people who had complaints . . . and then argue with them about each point they brought up.

Whenever I did something she didn't like, Principal One's response was always the same: to yell at me, telling me she could fire me any time she wanted. She'd even do this in front of colleagues, and worse—in front of the students and their parents. Principal One decided to retire after a year and a half of being an administrator because a friend of hers (also a principal in our district) suffered a heart attack, and Principal One had already been diagnosed with dangerously high blood pressure.

Principal Two

Principal Two was technically an "acting" principal in charge only of summer preparations during my third year. She was our assistant principal under Principal One. Prior to becoming an administrator, Principal Two had been an incredible kindergarten teacher—who just happened to be the only teacher in the school with an administrative credential when they needed an assistant principal.

Having a former kindergarten teacher who referred to all children as "cherubs" in charge of discipline for fifth grade inner-city kids turned out to be—to put it politely—ineffective. She would often just send kids right back to their teachers, with a note saying "Jimmy says he won't do it again," regardless of the infraction. I always felt that she had been pushed into the role of disciplinarian and was extremely unhappy because she'd rather be—and was better suited to—teaching and nurturing kindergartners.

Principal Three

An interim principal, Principal Three was one of my favorite colleagues, although he was at our school for only a few months. He came out of retirement when the district couldn't find a good principal for our school, and said he'd lead the school for as long as it took to find someone else.

I sincerely wish they had never found a replacement.

Principal Three was patient, kind, and soft-spoken, yet had a definite air of authority. He listened to teachers and was reasonable, intelligent, open to new ideas, and dedicated. He genuinely wanted what was best for the school. For example, he had two brand-new enthusiastic and talented, but totally inexperienced, teachers. To give them the best chance at success, he reduced their class size, understanding that their needs were different than the other teachers at that grade level.

Principal Four

Hired by a committee that included some of our best teachers, Principal Four worked at our school for about a year and a half. She was an African-American woman who claimed to be interested in improving communication with the large Latino population in the area. She even said she was taking Spanish classes to further communication between the two groups, which turned out to be a blatant lie. She seemed wonderful . . . until she wasn't.

During Principal Four's year and a half with us, the school's racial composition was about 50/50 black and Latino, with an additional small population of Southeast Asians. When the Latino parents wanted the school to spend some of its money on Spanish-language library books (a reasonable request, since we had classes that were taught in Spanish), several parents and staff members heard her say, "This is what you should do. You should go down to the corner, and open a tortilla stand. Then, with the money from the tortilla stand, you can buy some books in Spanish. Okay?"

After this incident, the teachers all signed a letter to the superintendent asking for her to be removed. She was—but the administration just transferred her to a different site in the same district.

Principal Five

After the disaster that was Principal Four, we thought that maybe, just maybe, the district might finally get a clue and give us a strong administrator. As luck had it, they picked someone who was nowhere near as bad as her predecessor, but who was still utterly inadequate.

They say that you can tell a lot about a person from their handshake. Principal Five's was telling; she had a limp fish handshake.

"Limp fish" turned out to be a good assessment of her management style as well. For example, when my classroom still hadn't been cleaned on the last day before school started, I told her there was no way my dirty classroom, with piles of furniture, would be ready for kids on the first day of school. She looked at a space right past my head, so she wasn't looking me in the eye and said, "I really don't know what you're going to do," and walked away.

In fact, this habit was what most people remember about Principal Five—her tendency to walk away when she knew you were trying to talk to her. She did that with kids, parents, and staff—just walked away like you weren't even there. Parents complained constantly about this habit.

In addition to her sub-par communication skills, Principal Five had completely ineffective discipline, and showed absolutely no engagement whatsoever with the school or any of the rest of us on campus. She left after one year, during which I never even saw her smile once.

Principal Six

Principal Six was *amazing*. Absolutely amazing. She was passionate and intelligent, she got things done, and she knew how to navigate all the counterproductive rules and procedures that came down from the district. What's more, she cared deeply for the kids and the parents, and even the staff.

She told the kids that they were in her heart and they were her family. She urged them to be proud of their heritage and to do their best to make their families and themselves proud. She never yelled at kids. Instead, she would remind us that our students had seen more violence and neglect in their short lifetimes than most of us ever would, so there was a reason for their behavior.

But that didn't mean she was going to let them slide either. She had high standards for students and didn't let them get away with bad behavior. This woman was simply *incredible*. But I think the excessive standardized testing and policies of our district got to her. After just one year, she left for another principal job in Berkeley. I didn't blame her because I knew what a hard job it was, working day in and day out at a school like ours. However, I admit that I felt abandoned when she left. It was hard to lose such a good leader.

Principal Seven

Principal Seven seemed good at first, only turning out to be a disappointment later. In the beginning, she appeared calm, collected, and competent. In many ways, she was. But she decided a few months into the year that the school was simply too difficult for her, and she'd find a different position. At that point, she more or less checked out and was unresponsive on all fronts, not answering emails or messages, and keeping her office door closed. She left after a year.

Principal Eight

My final principal was a former teacher with whom I'd taught side by side for seven years before he became an administrator. He was a great teacher; he seemed to be in the profession for the right reasons and loved the kids. What's more, as a teacher, he was willing to work hard and refused to capitulate to unreasonable demands from the district, being more interested in doing what was right than what was easy or expected.

But once he became the principal, his values seemed to shift. He fired teachers for no clear reason, or at least none he shared with the rest of us. Almost overnight, he became much more of a politician, saying whatever people wanted to hear without following through.

This one was particularly sad for me, as I'd had high hopes for his ability to lead the school.

Over time, I watched the never-ending game of musical principals at East Oakland Elementary take a serious toll on staff and students alike. I've seen schools in other tough neighborhoods thrive under the leadership of good, stable administrators—people who have managed to create excellent positive learning environments because they showed respect for the students and demanded respect in return, the right way—by earning it.

But creating that environment takes strong and consistent leadership—something we never had during my tenure at East Oakland Elementary. Strong, positive leadership could have been the catalyst to turn our school around, slowing teacher turnover and ensuring consistency for the students.

On the Wrong Track

When I started teaching in January 2000, our school had about 950 students: far too many children for the existing classrooms, but still well below the district's estimate of "full capacity" (closer to 1,100 students). To maximize the use of the space, the school went year-round and had four tracks. One track was always supposed to be on vacation, so only three-quarters of the students were in session at any given time. This made for a ridiculously complicated schedule: there would be three weeks when tracks A, B, and C were in school and D was on vacation. Then D would come back and track A would be on vacation, so tracks B, C, and D were in school. It went like that all year.

Besides the obvious logistical problems, there were other ramifications: one-quarter of the classes (two or three classes per track) had no permanent, dedicated classroom. Instead, they had "roving classrooms," and every three weeks, the teacher had to pack up all of his or her stuff, all student work, *everything*, and move to another classroom inhabited by a teacher who was on vacation. I had a roving classroom my first year as a teacher.

The school gave us exactly one hour of paid time to move everything and get organized in the new room. Even the teachers who were in nominally stable classrooms had to make room for the rovers to move into their classrooms (rather like squatters) just as they were leaving for vacation. To make matters worse, all the teachers were so stressed out by the lack of support and the frenetic schedule that no one had the time or energy to help anyone else move. When it was your turn to uproot your entire class, you were completely on your own.

Across the board, teachers are exceptionally territorial about their classrooms. I found that few were willing to share with others. The permanent teachers were supposed to provide storage space for the roving teachers, and I think one teacher once gave me most of a drawer and part of a cupboard. Most wouldn't let me hang anything up, put anything in cupboards, or use bookshelves. In addition, I was told not to use their things.

While the tracking schedule was always difficult when three tracks were in session, there was one more complication: the tracks' schedules were short about two weeks. These days had to be made up, so all four tracks were in session—in any space available. Once I had to teach in the auditorium and, another time, in the auditorium lobby. There were no desks in the auditorium, so the first-graders sat at adult-sized tables in metal folding chairs, with no heat and hardly any light. The challenges were exacerbated in the winter when rain prevented the kids from going outside for recess, and we shared the cavernous, echoing space with all the third, fourth, and fifth graders, who had little supervision and nothing to do. Needless to say, the environment was not exactly conducive to teaching my first graders.

In my year with a roving classroom, my poor first graders never did get the schedule down or consistently remember which classroom we were in at what time. We'd line up as a class to go into the building, but the students would make their way toward three different class-rooms as soon as we started walking. Other teachers would have to call me and say that one of my very confused students was in their classroom.

Although I believe the practice of roving classrooms is now obsolete in Oakland due to declining enrollment, it was a defining part of my abrupt entry into teaching. At the time, I thought of the practice more or less as new teacher hazing. In retrospect, it seems more like abject insanity.

Having Your Lunch and Eating It Too

The teachers' mandated duty-free lunch was a point of constant conten-tion between the teachers and the administrators. In our contracts with the district, we were guaranteed a thirty-minute lunch period with *zero* responsibilities.

Never mind that none of us ever experienced this kind of a lunch. Thirty minutes wasn't enough to do much of anything, and 95 percent of us spent it making copies, correcting papers, calling about field trips, and calling parents. Nonetheless, that was *our* time, and we needed it, so we fought for it.

Lunchtime for teachers gets eroded easily. Sometimes there were "optional" lunch meetings—or, to be more specific, "voluntary, but highly recommended." These were also known as "you'll look bad if you don't go; we can't legally force you to, but we'll never forget if you don't" lunch meetings. And then there were the "right before lunch and might spill over into your lunchtime, but we'll pretend not to notice" meetings.

During one such meeting, the administrator said, "I can't *make* you stay through your duty-free lunch, but does anyone have any objection to staying?" That was a tough moment for me. I certainly had an objection: that I already worked much too hard for too little pay and not enough prep time or respect, and I wasn't going to give up my measly thirty-minute lunchtime for a silly meeting that wasn't worth my time.

But I knew if I objected, I would never hear the end of it. I'd be classified as not being a team player—the one who didn't want to work hard and just took the easy way out.

So I lied.

I said that I had copies to make and children's parents to call and field trips to check on. All true, but not necessarily things I would do during lunchtime. I didn't say that I just needed downtime because I was tired. I didn't say I needed time to be away from kids or to just *eat*. I didn't say that I needed to go to the bathroom, or that I might have wanted a few minutes to make a personal call or catch up on paying my bills or email some friends, as this was an unpaid lunch period.

I also didn't stand up and scream that the administration was making me crazy and no wonder teachers burned out in California—and specifically in Oakland—because they couldn't even have *thirty lousy minutes* to themselves!

None of that would have helped. So I lied.

May Ms. Harris Be Excused Today?

In addition to the inconvenience of teachers needing time to eat, the inevitability of us occasionally falling ill during the school year was a sore spot with administrators. Many teachers feel guilty for calling in sick—not just from the overt or tacit disapproval of administrators but also from self-imposed guilt. I often felt as though I were deserting my own children when I needed to call in sick. Most teachers I know feel it's easier to go to school sick than to make plans for a substitute and then deal with the aftermath. But then those sick teachers pass their germs to everybody else—like me, for instance.

One of our revolving principals sent me home one day when I was trying to "grin and bear it" through a painful injury. She happened to have an extra substitute and told me, "We in education buy into guilt too much and end up not taking care of ourselves." I wish I had taken those words to heart better then. If I had, perhaps I wouldn't have fallen so terribly ill toward the end of my time at the school.

Taking those words to heart, though, was difficult given the mixed messages we received. Even though reasonable sentiments like this were occasionally offered, they were often proven to be just talk, with little action to back them up. In this case, the next time I was sick—with strep throat—that *same principal* told me that if I wasn't really committed, I should get out of education.

I think the school building itself played a part in my recurring illnesses. I taught in a portable classroom for five or six years, and during those years, I thought I had developed really bad asthma. I was sick a lot, including an annual case of bronchitis, which turned into at least a month of illness-induced asthma, complete with trips to the emergency room. After I left the portable classroom, these symptoms vanished—no coughing, no wheezing, and no respiratory distress.

Shortly after I left that classroom, I saw an article about formaldehyde being found in particleboard, medium-density fiberboard, and plywood. The article cited formaldehyde as a cause not only of cancer, but also respiratory allergies, asthma, coughing, wheezing, and chest tightness. The portable classrooms were made of plywood, fiberboard, and particleboard. A perfect trifecta, likely explaining many of my symptoms that year. I shudder to think what daily exposure may have done to my students, with their still-developing lungs.

In my fifth year of teaching, I sprained my ankle at school. I didn't file for workers' compensation even though it happened on campus, because I had good insurance and it was easier to deal with the injury that way. I tried my best to teach my third graders on crutches, which was almost impossible, as I was constantly walking around to explain concepts, check on students, head off behavior problems, and walk the kids from one activity to another. But I took as few days off as possible.

The administration was absolutely inflexible in making *any* accommodations. I still had to teach PE on crutches, even when other teachers volunteered to do it for me. I still had to walk my students across the yard, despite these offers of help from my colleagues. I tried to schedule all my doctor's appointments after school hours, but of course we had meetings. So sometimes I had to choose between missing the school day and missing a meeting, which then earned me a lecture either way.

When I did take a couple of days off because of the excruciating pain in my arms and back from doing everything on crutches, I got another lecture from my principal about how I really needed to be committed to these kids—when, by the way, I was the second teacher in seniority at our school at age twenty-eight. If my longevity didn't show commitment to the kids, I don't know what would. Teacher retention was a huge problem in this district, and this experience gave me a glimpse of why.

Despite lack of support from the administration, I rarely felt unappreciated by my students. Once while my kids were in the middle of a test, a former student came in to visit.

"Juan," I said, "you're not supposed to be in this building during testing." He said, "Oh, I just wanted to bring you something . . . for Teachers' Day," and handed me a well-loved stuffed Taco Bell dog that said "*Feliz Navidad, amigos*" when you squeezed it.

I wasn't even his teacher anymore, but he had thought of me. When I look back and wonder how I lasted as long as I did under the untenable conditions at the school, the answers is always: the kids.

A Culture of Blame and Distrust

Between the never-ending game of musical principals, the practice of roving classrooms, and the general lack of consideration for the health and well-being of teachers, it's no small wonder that staff turnover was astronomically high.

It didn't help that some principals would threaten teachers with comments like, "I can have your job at any time, you know!" even in cases where we hadn't done anything wrong. Although these threats may have been just a way of blowing off steam, they were examples of poor leadership: counterproductive, stress-inducing, and just plain mean.

All of this stress was exacerbated by the unreasonably strict schedules we were expected to follow and the people from the district who would drop in to ensure compliance. This micro-managing required us to be on the exact right page for that day of the curriculum—ignoring the fact that students might be particularly interested in one subject or have experienced something traumatic that knocked us off schedule. Every one of us was reprimanded at some point—gently or otherwise—for not following the district-wide schedule *to the minute*.

No Child Left Behind (the education initiative passed during George W. Bush's presidency) made everything worse. I remember hearing Bush's Secretary of State Condoleezza Rice talk about how our government was setting benchmarks for Iraq to measure their progress in governing themselves. She added that Iraq would not be punished for failing to meet these benchmarks, because that wouldn't be helpful or productive.

And yet the same administration punished teachers and students— yes, they used the word *sanctions*—for not meeting benchmarks on our tests. When our school did not meet these benchmarks, we had teacher's aides cut, our field trip budget cut, and finally our school "reconstituted"—meaning that all of the teachers were forced to reapply for their jobs.

Over time, my stress level from work grew to the point that I constantly felt exhausted and yet had trouble sleeping at night. A vague feeling of dread about school persisted—an irrational fear that I would be "in trouble," no doubt built up by the poor working conditions and the unfortunate treatment my colleagues and I received from our administrators and the district.

By then I was tenured, so I knew the possibility of being fired was highly unlikely unless I *really* messed up. I could have been given an involuntary transfer within the district, but not until the end of a school year. And as a friend said, "What are they going to do, move you to a *hard* school?" Still, the feeling persisted: I was at constant risk of censure without reasonable cause.

I was a professional with extensive and ongoing training for my job, and I was quite good at it when left alone to do it. Being monitored and frequently reprimanded to such an unreasonable extent didn't make me a better teacher. It made me a bitter, burned-out, tired, awake-at-four-o'clock-in-the-morning-and-thinking-about-other-career-possibilities teacher.

The pervasive atmosphere of blame and punishment probably wasn't unique to my district and probably wasn't intentional. I imagine that principals have an immense amount of pressure on them and that some—or most—of them deal with it the only way they know how: to take it out on teachers.

But teachers can't last in that kind of environment. And neither can the kids we teach.

CHAPTER 4

THE PERILS OF TEACHING TO THE TEST

"*Accountability makes no sense when it undermines the larger goals of education.*"

—DIANE RAVITCH,
   The Death and Life of the Great American School System: How Testing and Choice Are Undermining Education

American public education has used standardized testing as a benchmark measure of both student and school performance for generations. Choosing what to measure, though, ends up determining not only what our children will learn, but also, specifically, what they will not. In 2001, the George W. Bush administration enacted the No Child Left Behind (NCLB) Act, which stressed reading comprehension and math, while social studies, science, art, music, and other "non-essential" subjects were often simply ignored.

Teachers were encouraged to *only* teach the subjects that would be on the test.

This means that even if a "non-essential" topic stayed on the syllabus, we were not given sufficient time to teach it properly. Ironically, these "frivolous" subjects were often the ones that engaged students in learning, taught critical thinking and creativity, and boosted self-esteem. In my experience, this shortsighted prioritization led to countless missed opportunities in the classroom.

While there were good intentions behind NCLB (e.g., ensuring accountability and qualified teachers, and making sure that all students received a quality education), the draconian implementation of it caused more problems than it solved. Among other provisions, the new law linked federal funding for individual schools directly to their students' performance on state-mandated tests.

In other words, schools that did well on the tests were rewarded financially, while schools that did poorly faced a variety of sanctions. Not surprisingly, this reliance on test scores struck a blow against the financial survival of already underfunded public schools in lower-income areas (which are far more reliant on federal funds than schools in wealthier areas). Where test scores were not high enough, some schools were even "reconstituted," (replacing most or all of a school's staff) or closed altogether.

While NCLB was eventually repealed under the Obama administration in 2015, the years that it was in place were extremely damaging to many children. With its narrow focus on the "essential core" of phonics, math, and basic reading comprehension, NCLB did a real disservice to the cohorts of students who experienced it. For students who succeeded in these basics, there were few enrichment opportunities to engage them in creative pursuits or disciplines that would give them a broader education. Moreover, with its emphasis on achieving "grade-level readiness," the students who surpassed that mark were essentially left to languish on their own.

But the system was no better for children who struggled with the basics. Supplementary topics like nature, science, art, music, and literature can provide the needed "hook" to capture a student's love of learning or introduce her to a potential life-long passion or career. When children of under-resourced families are less likely to have parents who can take them to concerts, museums, or the zoo, it is incumbent on our educational system to help fill—rather than widen—this gap.

In my years of teaching, I have seen time and time again how these "supplementary" topics are the ones that capture students' enthusiasm. Good performance, whether on the tests or in life, isn't a product of rote learning: it results from engagement, critical thinking, and a belief in one's self and one's abilities. These intangibles have been hollowed out by adherence to only the core subjects, much to the detriment of so many students.

What good does it do the next generation to focus exclusively on educational basics when we carve out everything that allows them to truly connect and engage with what we're trying to teach them?

A Natural Approach to Critical Thinking Skills

Although it was not present as a topic in the NCLB curriculum, there was clearly a need for my students to learn about nature. This became apparent when I led a trash pickup at a park, and almost every child came up to me with a leaf or a stick and asked, "Does this count as trash?" "No," I replied again and again. "That's nature."

"Teacher," they'd say, "how that nature? That's trash!"

So I was understandably excited when our reading program included a unit on City Wildlife. Here was a way to sneak in nature content and build on the kids' natural curiosity about plants and animals. When we began the unit, I could tell I was building on a shaky foundation and would first need to define the term. For instance, I had to clarify that zoo animals do not count as city wildlife, because they are no longer wild—

they're being taken care of by humans. Likewise, tigers in the wild didn't count because they don't live in cities. The kids finally reached a definition along the lines of "plants or animals that live in our city and survive without being taken care of."

Of course, the reading program didn't take inner-city schools into consideration. The teacher's edition specifically said that cats and dogs are *not* city wildlife. Really? What about all the feral pit bulls running around East Oakland? As the kids said, "Nobody be taking care of them and they be surviving!" Questions like these always led to interesting discussions and the chance for young students to learn to form their own opinions.

Now on a roll and thinking well outside the box of what the textbook publishers anticipated, one of the kids took the definition to its logical conclusion and said, "So homeless people is city wildlife, too! Don't nobody be taking care of them or giving them a place to live and they still alive." Leave it to the kids to point out that we have people in our cities who aren't treated much better than the pigeons and sewer rats.

In these cracks and spaces in between the intentions of the unit, however, the kids were developing their critical thinking skills. Moments like these that give the kids the opportunity to recognize the choices that our society is making and reflect on whether or not they themselves would make the same or different choices are a key exercise in character formation.

Unfortunately, such moments become all too rare in the classroom when the teacher is tied to a stringent curriculum schedule.

Weird Science

Many people may find it shocking—even horrifying—to learn that, under NCLB, science was for many years considered an unessential rather than core subject. Happily, our district just happened to have the perfect companion science activity for the City Wildlife unit: dissecting owl pellets. A teacher only had to make a request for supplies, and in a surprising display of efficiency for a district where most requests languished for weeks or months, the owl pellet guy showed up the very next day.

He brought a class set of owl pellets and tweezers, along with a video that showed how owls eat and then regurgitate pellets made of whatever parts of their prey they're unable to digest. The kids loved it because it's gross. We teachers loved it because, in dissecting the owl pellets, the students had a tangible experience of hands-on scientific discovery, something they would remember far more vividly than reading a book or just watching a video.

Unfortunately, many teachers did not take advantage of the owl pellets or the other science units available because there just wasn't time to teach them. Worse, at many schools, the administrators reprimanded teachers who taught science (or art, or anything else not on the test) because it didn't "count for anything"—toward test preparation, anyway. I have heard that, thankfully, this changed after I left, and that teachers were more often encouraged to teach science, and even given relevant materials.

"States of Matter" was another engaging third-grade science unit with a hands-on component. And like owl pellets, it was often skipped so that more time could be spent on the subjects assessed on the year-end standardized tests.

Fortunately, I had a secret weapon to preserve student enthusiasm for science: Mr. Jackson, an intrepid mechanic who was a big believer in the importance of science experiments in the classroom. Over a series of classroom visits and field trip chaperoning, he had demonstrated a knack for connecting with the students. So when the kids heard he would be coming back to lead a session on "States of Matter," they were excited.

On the appointed day, Mr. Jackson arrived carrying a camping stove, a big pot, a glass bottle, dry ice, some candles, a jar, balloons, baking soda, and vinegar. Seeing such a wide assortment of interesting things, the kids knew that science was going to be fun and made more of an effort than usual to behave and stay in their seats, despite their obvious, squirming excitement.

Mr. Jackson started by explaining the difference in the molecular activity of solids, liquids, and gases, all the while using the kids themselves as examples of molecules moving at different speeds. He showed them that air is actually a substance by making carbon dioxide gas with baking soda and vinegar in a jar. As the students watched, the invisible gas put out the candle flames. To them, it was like magic, and in turn, that made learning about science magical.

There were all sorts of other experiments and demonstrations that day, including blowing up a balloon with the carbon dioxide gas from the vinegar and baking soda reaction and creating a vacuum inside a plastic soda bottle.

But the best part, of course, was the dry ice. Mr. Jackson explained what dry ice was, but mostly he just showed the kids how to play with it. We saw the fog created by dry ice in a pot with hot water. The kids called it "the witches' brew" and came up to run their hands through it. Then he added dish soap, and a "bubble fountain" erupted.

They loved it. After that, the kids begged for more science, especially experiments. I began to use science as a reward, instead of offering a class party or extra recess, and it was just as effective as a means of motivating hard work and good behavior.

For many children (and us adults, too), there's something about the hands-on aspect of science that makes it different and more special than many other subjects or rote learning—something that helps young students buy into school and into their own learning process.

As our elected officials and corporate leaders bemoan the American slide in global competitiveness and the lack of graduates with science, technology, engineering, and mathematics (STEM) skills, perhaps they should consider emphasizing science in the classroom.

Sculpting Young Minds

It may be surprising that science was disappearing, but it's no secret that art has long been on the chopping block in elementary schools. I wish the people cutting the budget could see how detrimental this is to our students. On those days when I was able to work the arts into my class, the kids thrived—even if we just spent a short time on something creative.

It's obvious that kids *need* art. After just one class, whether it was on color theory, book construction, or painting, the children went from being disengaged and robotic to being excited and confident. They began noticing colors and shapes around them and looking forward to future art projects. Even something as simple as learning that blue and yellow paint mixed together make green paint captured their imaginations and interest, spurring them to come up with ideas of new color combinations and how to make different shades of green.

My favorite destination for art field trips was MOCHA (Museum of Children's Art) in downtown Oakland. It's a fascinating place for children and adults alike, with warm and talented teachers, and a wide repertoire of lessons that appeal to children of all ages. I took nearly all of my classes there, and each one had a thoroughly positive experience, because the teachers who work there know children as well as they know art.

On one trip, my students made sculptures out of recycled materials. Each child got a hot glue gun, a pressed wood base, and access to all sorts of recycled objects: water bottles, wood pieces, crocheted fruits, cinnamon sticks, pine cones, plastic tops, and all sorts of other things I couldn't even begin to identify.

This project made the field trip a resounding success. For a full ninety minutes, the kids didn't glue things to each other, burn each other with the hot glue guns, throw things at each other, put each other down, or even call their own sculptures stupid. They just created, and they were totally absorbed in what they were doing and in having a great time. Later, on the BART trip home, the kids received many compliments on their art projects from passersby, giving them the validation that kids naturally crave from adults.

The effects of such field trips lasted longer than just those single days. The students tended to talk about field trips they'd taken for at least a week afterward, reliving the highlights of the trip and hoping out loud that they could go on another one soon. Often, children who did not do well in school excelled at art projects and adored these trips. Art helps children learn in many ways, including developing fine motor skills, spatial intelligence, and self-expression. The arts also provide an outlet for kids who aren't able to express themselves in other ways.

I always wanted to do these kinds of art projects in the classroom, but the barriers were too daunting. In the classroom, I was on my own, whereas at MOCHA, I was paired with another trained teacher and had the support of the chaperones (a mix of students' parents and my friends). My classroom also wasn't stocked with art supplies the way that MOCHA was, and the luxury of MOCHA's dedicated art space made the cleanup process more manageable. Children wielding paint is an overwhelming idea for the teacher who will be in charge of clean-up.

But realistically, my administration's disapproval of time spent on anything other than test prep was the biggest stumbling block. I would have been reprimanded by the vast majority of my various principals for spending time on such a thing. A rare field trip was acceptable, but spending class time teaching art when we could have been spending one more hour preparing for the test was frowned upon.

Sorely Tested

If NCLB took away much of the fun of school in the form of science, nature, music, art, and literature, what did it offer in return? In a word, stress.

The state standardized testing was a source of great anxiety for the students. For third graders under NCLB, there were approximately fourteen hours of testing, spread over a period of two weeks. The total time of this test was longer than the SAT taken by high school students, or the MCAT, LSAT, or GRE tests taken by college seniors or graduates for admission to graduate or professional school.

One student, Lamar, took his test standing up because we had two parts that day, and after the first part he just couldn't sit any more. One girl fell asleep on her test and left drool marks on it. A couple of others left tear stains, and I even had a friend whose student urinated on his test.

The state standardized test was only one part of the regimen. The district had its own assessments and didn't always plan them out too carefully. During my time there, we were asked not once, but *twice*, to test students on math material that hadn't been covered in the district-mandated pacing guide. In the case of certain word problems and some geometry questions, the material was supposed to be taught several weeks *after* the tests were due.

The kicker was that the *same department* made the schedules for these lesson plans *and* for the tests. No wonder the students felt inadequate when the district's lack of organization meant they were being set up to fail.

Meanwhile, one of our administrators added another assessment from a math curriculum that was reported to be good but that we weren't actually using. That begged the question of why we were taking its test. One teacher doggedly asked, "So . . . will we be using this assessment to drive instruction?" The answer was no. "Will we get a chance to be trained in this curriculum?" No again. "Will we get to teach this curriculum at all?" No, we were not using this math curriculum. He asked once more, "So, we're just giving the assessment, even though we're not using the curriculum and we don't know what the assessment will show us?"

Yes. The answer was yes.

The kids weren't the only ones who suffered from stress on account of the tests. To cope with added strain of the never-ending and sometimes nonsensical tests, I decided to make a gratitude list for the state standardized tests. It was a short list:

1. The school gives us enough pencils for every kid, *and* they're pre-sharpened.
2. The kids get a snack, so they're not hungry until lunch. (Well, for the first few days they get a snack, until the school inevitably runs out of snack money.)
3. I can lock the door and no one comes in to tell me I'm off schedule or that I have no student work on display.

The students' behavior was especially squirrely on testing days. In a single day during one year's testing period, I had one child get sent home for fighting, three more whose mothers were called, and seven more who got in some sort of trouble. All of it started with the test. The kids felt stupid—like they didn't measure up—feelings reinforced by taking what seemed like endless assessments.

One year, I gave my students special "magic pencils" on the first day of testing. I was mostly kidding, but the kids bought into it. They asked how I had made them magic and told me the magic pencils really did make them smarter. It seemed to help allay their anxieties at least a little bit. Despite my best efforts, however, the tests dragged the kids down. I got a note from one girl that read: "I hate the test so munch the test make people sad and mad that's why I hate test because there are answers that are really hard and stupid."

This student didn't used to feel that way about tests. All the assessments she had taken up until that point, including reading, math, and spelling, she saw as actually being fun. She *liked* taking tests, usually did well on them, and never freaked out. But the school had put so much pressure on the kids about this test in particular that everyone felt it because the stakes were so high.

I did get another nice note from the girl who hated the test "so munch." She wrote, "I love you and Tiger very munch because you are very nice to me in my heart."

I guess that could have been number four on my gratitude list. Thank goodness for Tiger, our class pet that year. When that little gecko came out to watch the kids during the test, everyone relaxed a little.

What's the Point?

When the kids in my class would express frustration about the testing, I always told them that the people who made the tests "didn't know third graders." I did this to help them feel better, but I think it has to be true. Anyone who has spent time with children understands that trying to make them sit still for hours on end is a terrible idea and won't reflect the best that young students are capable of.

In addition to the effect on the students, the problems in the testing methodology impacted the school and teachers. At least at that time, to the best of my understanding, the scores of all the students enrolled in a class during the testing period were attributed to both the school and the teacher, regardless of how long the students had been there. Therefore, if a teacher had a fairly transient class, the test scores would not reflect his or her actual teaching.

We did have a lot of students move in and out during the year due to custody changes, homelessness, and residential changes. One year, when I had twenty students, my top five moved the day before the standardized testing window. In exchange, I received a student who had not been enrolled in school for most of the year due to homelessness, a student who had moved to the United States from Mexico City the week prior, a child who was changing schools because he was such a "behavior problem," and two fairly run-of-the-mill low achieving students. If the testing window had been two weeks earlier, our school's third grade scores would have been significantly higher.

Another quirk of the testing system under NCLB was that the tests didn't measure improvement but strictly whether or not students were at grade level. If a boy began his third grade year reading at a preschool level and ended at a second grade level, his performance didn't count as a success because he was still below grade level. But if another student began the year at a fourth grade level and ended at a fourth grade level, she would be a success, as she was above grade level, even though she had made zero progress during the year.

The unintended (I hope) consequence of this testing scheme is that I was told repeatedly to ignore the kids who were far below grade level, because *they wouldn't improve enough*.

In other words, as a third-grade teacher, if a child could not read at all, I wasn't supposed to put any extra time into that child, even if that time meant that he or she could improve, learn to read, and end the year at a first-grade level. While such a feat would make a huge difference in the education and life of that child, it wouldn't help our school's test scores improve. More than one principal told me some variation of "We'll help them [the children working far below grade level] after we can keep our school from closing." Unfortunately, it would by then be far too late to help the specific children I was worried about. Gifted children were similarly ignored, as they were already going to do fine on the test.

Even from an economic standpoint, the kind of testing that kids have endured under NCLB doesn't make sense. Testing is far from cheap for schools, either in time or in money. If we spent the equivalent energy and resources on art, literature, field trips, science, and music that we do on testing, our students would be much better off.

If we want an accurate assessment of how our children, teachers, and schools are performing, we should at least structure the tests to fit within the curriculum and the attention span of the students, and modify the scoring so that teachers and schools are evaluated by the improvement of the students they taught, not simply whether the students who happen to be sitting in their classroom for the testing period meet a "performing at grade level" metric.

Our pursuit of accountability has made us lose sight of our true goals: to educate each student according to his or her needs, to awaken the joy of learning, and to inspire each child to make it a life-long journey.

CHAPTER 5

THE VALUE OF MUTUAL RESPECT

"*Ms. Harris don't play.***"**

— THIRD-GRADE STUDENT

Effective teaching requires the respect and trust of the students. Understandably, kids who have been abandoned or betrayed by the adults in their lives have an especially difficult time learning to respect and trust new adults. Therefore, establishing authority in the classroom with disadvantaged kids in poorer neighborhoods, like the one where I taught, can be particularly challenging.

Children's sense of self is directly tied to the subtle (or not so subtle) messages they receive from adults. Too often with the kids I taught, those messages came in the form of neglect and lack of access to resources, with devastating consequences for my students' sense of self-worth.

Heartbreakingly, some of my students had been convinced—by age eight or nine—that they were stupid and worthless. DaShon was one such child. Though he had been held back in first grade, he was very smart—one of those kids who is almost too smart for his own good, in fact. He understood more higher-level concepts than most other students in his grade.

Due to the backlog of students waiting to be assessed for learning disabilities, DaShon hadn't been tested, but my armchair diagnosis was a processing problem that made it difficult for him to read and write. After much hard work and patience, and with more support, he finally started believing in himself. One of my proudest moments that year was when he received the "most improved writer" award for the entire third grade.

Here are some samples of his writing from October, January, and March. Each of these writing samples was supposed to be a paragraph.

October:
"to mack a friend isto be nice and to shar and to play with thim sumtimes give thim toys."

January:
"It's adout a place where a lot of ducks lives. The boy told his dad and thay wint to the wood ond the boy wated to tall hisfriend odou want he sow it was a lot of baby ducks. and the story the dad was biger thin the mom."

March:

"The author wanted us to know, that your family is more important than money, because you would not be in this wrld and you not be, at a fun ealss like thas school and as much fun in thas Grass thas, so fun! to be in and you can Read and rite and do math and it as a lot of stuff to do."

Yes, we still had a lot of work to do as of March, but his writing was already *so* much better.

DaShon was one of my favorites. In his case, ironically, his high intelligence actually got in the way of his ability to learn. This was a child who managed to outsmart his second grade teacher—a rookie with abominable classroom management skills, and who lasted only one year on East Oakland Elementary's faculty. DaShon quickly calculated that he could run the classroom and proceeded to do so. He became a ringleader, roping other kids into coloring on the floor with crayons, swearing at the teacher, or joining him in his overblown, cartoon-style temper tantrums.

These behavioral reports confused me, because for the two years I had known DaShon, he was always very respectful to me, even when his teacher sent him to me for a time out.

I requested that DaShon be placed in my third grade class, and on the first day, we had a chat. I told him I had noticed his behavior in second grade and thought he had probably outsmarted his teacher. He said, "Yeah, I was smarter than her." I agreed with him, which I think surprised him.

Then I leaned forward and looked him in the eye. "DaShon," I said, "you are not smarter than I am."

"No, no," he answered, "I don't think I am."

"You are very smart," I clarified, "but so am I. You will not be in charge of this classroom this year. I will."

"You're right," he said.

I never had a problem with him all year. Not once. He worked hard. I think he finally learned that he was smart. And the next year he had an excellent fourth-grade teacher who has stayed in touch with him and mentored him.

In order to learn, DaShon really just needed to know that his teacher was competent, in control, and someone he could respect. Given his success in derailing his second grade class, he may have been an extreme case—but at their core, other kids aren't much different: all children need respect.

Kids can tell when adults don't respect them, and they respond accordingly. I've found that to be successful in the classroom, it's just as vital for teachers to respect our students as it is to win their respect.

Winning Hearts and Minds

During the time I was a classroom teacher, I found the loyalty of my students to be a complicated subject. To this day, I don't claim a total understanding of the psychology of this, but I have a working theory based on my experiences.

When I first started teaching in Oakland, it was January. The class I took over had already been through *six* teachers that year. Their original teacher reportedly had a nervous breakdown, suffering panic attacks every time he arrived at school. After him, they'd burned through five substitute teachers.

Understandably, the kids were skeptical about how long I'd last at that school. They would often ask when I was leaving because they expected it. In their experience, teachers—especially young, idealistic, white ones—came and went all the time.

So why should I be any different?

Gradually, though, things changed. The kids began to ask things like, "What school will you work at when you leave?" Or they'd say, "I hope my brother be in your class before you leave." At that point, they were simply wondering what the duration of my stay would be rather than assuming my departure to be imminent. But they were also beginning to express how sad they'd be when I inevitably left and to consider how we might stay in touch.

Over time, they started to tell other kids, "Ms. Harris has always been here." Or, "She ain't gonna leave us." They would make ambitious plans about how they would come visit when they were in high school, or how their kids would someday have me as a teacher.

Once it became clear that I wasn't in a rush to leave, the kids' parents and guardians also warmed up to me. Whereas at first, they deferred to me and spoke to me in a noticeably formal way, they at last began to visibly let their guard down in my presence. Parents began to bring me food, talk to me about topics beyond just their kids or school, ask me about my life, and treat me more like a peer instead of dismissing me as an educated and privileged white teacher trying to "save" inner-city youth (although this initial attitude was understandable, given their previous experience with many white teachers, either their children's or their own).

At that point, my students' parents told me directly that they didn't feel like I was all that different from them, that I wasn't like "those other white people," and that I wasn't trying to just "be a do-gooder." No longer wary of me, many of the mothers and grandmothers I often talked to stopped worrying if their grammar wasn't correct, or if they didn't speak English well. I felt honored when they started telling me about the hard parts of their lives in addition to the celebrations and successes.

What had changed? I think the parents finally realized I wasn't there because of educational ideals or a sense of owing a debt to society, or anything else that wouldn't last—but quite simply because I loved their children. Our school was lucky to have some wonderful teachers over the years, but sadly, this mindset about teaching was rare. When the parents found a teacher who shared that motivation, they responded with enthusiasm. (The administration, alas, did not.)

The hard truth is that idealism gets squashed pretty quickly in teaching, and when it does, the teachers who are there for the wrong—if well-intentioned—reasons leave or mentally check out. Frankly, it's hard to blame them. But when you love a particular group of children dearly, it's much harder to walk away.

As I was accepted into the community, I established authority with the students and they repaid me with loyalty.

Kids with a reputation for being disrespectful and destroying school property would reprimand other students who dared to disrespect me. Because I stuck around and gave the kids a chance to know, respect, and—in some cases—love me, I was different in their eyes than many teachers they were used to.

The Snowball Effect

Once I had won them over with staying power and mutual respect, the kids started backing me up—even to each other. I would hear them say things like, "Oh, you better get in your seat, 'cause you know she ain't playing. She *will* call your mama," and "Girl, you know you don't talk to the teacher that way!" The best one, though, was "You know she care about you even when she mad, and she only upset 'cause she want you to get your education."

This respect effectively snowballed, translating into an incredible amount of authority. Sometimes, I didn't have to say anything; I could just give "the look" (every teacher knows it!), or count to three, or hold out my hand for whatever they weren't supposed to have in theirs, and the child would—albeit reluctantly—fall in line.

As a white woman from the suburbs, my lone source of street cred was simply sticking it out in that community for so many years. That made all the difference. Commitment and consistency, along with love for the students, made it possible to overcome many cultural and racial barriers.

Establishing mutual trust and respect with my students garnered me a few unexpected benefits, too. I had one student who even the other inner-city kids were afraid of—to the point that they would cross the street to get away from him. I had to tell him that he couldn't call me "Blood" or "Dog," as I was his teacher and this was disrespectful. He tried hard to respect my wishes. Once when he walked into my classroom, we had a one-sided "conversation" that went something like this:

> Andrew: [*kind of cocky*] What up, blood? [*looks at me, and upon seeing my expression, says quickly*]: I mean, what up, dog? [*now looking really flustered*] I mean, what up, mama? [*now totally embarrassed*] I mean, what up, teacher? [*Andrew sits down and puts his head down, having totally confused himself.*]

The authority I had developed enabled me to command respect without saying one word, and this helped me begin to understand the role I had at the school. However, I knew I had made it when the school custodian asked how long I'd been there. I was thirty-one at the time, and had been there seven years. That made me the longest-lasting teacher on staff at that time.

He said, "Girl, you the OG [short for "Original Gangster," a term for someone who's been around a while] of this school! You seen it all!"

One student stuck up for me when he heard another teacher disparage me. He said, "Don't you be talking 'bout my teacher! Don't nobody talk about my teacher!" In that place, I figured if I were upsetting many of the adults and had earned the kids' loyalty, I must have been doing something right.

On Walkabout

Field trips present a particular challenge for maintaining the obedience and safety of a class.

My class often took BART (Bay Area Rapid Transit) for field trips. The walk from school to the train station (about three-quarters of a mile) was daunting for children completely unaccustomed to exercise (a common situation, since their neighborhoods were generally too dangerous for outdoor play) and their equally sedentary chaperones.

Kids are funny, though. Even as they whined about their feet hurting, the minute I said, "Race to the corner," they ran as fast as they could.

We passed all sorts of interesting people and things on the way to the BART station. Remember, this was *not* a good part of the city. We saw women working street corners, drug deals, dogfights, overflowing sewers . . . you get the idea. During my second year of teaching, the kids told me which street to skip to avoid the local crack house.

The train station itself was not without its own dangers. Between the risk of falling onto a track, or being squished by a train or electrocuted by the third rail, we always had a serious class talk about behavior expectations before any field trip. I covered the key rules: stay with the group, don't get ahead of the teacher, and don't run two at a time through the ticket gate (because that causes major problems on the way out). Perhaps the most important rule of all was not to get close to the edge of the BART platform.

Like most public transit platforms, the edges of BART train platforms are painted with a cautionary yellow stripe. My class rule forbade not merely touching the yellow stripe—students couldn't go anywhere *close* to the yellow stripe. Dangers of this magnitude had a clear consequence: I informed the kids that if I caught them going near the edge, not only would I ban them from future field trips in my class, but I would also encourage their fourth and fifth grade teachers to do the same.

With that much buildup of "forbidden fruit," of course I had one student eager to test me. There he was, walking on the yellow stripe as if it were a tightrope—*on the edge of the platform.*

Before I could get to him, one of the chaperones—an extremely responsive mom—grabbed him by the arm and started yelling, telling him exactly what she would do if she were his mother.

True to my word, I never let that child go on another field trip; it was too dangerous. In future classes, I always included his story as a precautionary tale, and I never had another student test me in the same way. The kids would say, "And did he get to go on any more field trips?" When I said no, they listened carefully and stayed far away from the tracks and the edge of the platform.

While threats were part of the arsenal, I had another trick up my sleeve to ensure the behavior of the students on the BART trains was always exceptionally good. It is a generalization, but children in extremely under-resourced areas, especially those raised by only a mom or a grandmother, take their mothers very seriously. That's the reason the ubiquitous "yo mama" jokes will get inner-city kids so riled up; insulting their mom is the worst thing you can possibly do.

But there's also a way to use this to your advantage.

Here's what I did: I made it a point to ask the kids how many of their parents took BART or the bus to work or school or appointments. Immediately, everyone would start talking at once, telling me stories about where their mothers work, go to school, or have appointments. Then I asked them how they would feel if there were kids on the BART train who were acting up, yelling and pushing when their mothers were trying to rest while going to or from work.

They were shocked that any kids would even *think* of acting in such an irresponsible manner when *their mother* was on the train and tired!

Bingo.

That's all it took. After that, they reminded each other to behave. Occasionally, I would have to say, "Remember, somebody's mom could be on the train and she might be tired," and they would act like angels.

The Single Most Important Thing a Teacher Can Do

In a 2011 Tavis Smiley documentary about juvenile incarceration called *Too Important to Fail*, one featured student recounted a time in fourth grade when his teacher told him he would never amount to anything. He said that after that, he simply gave up.

I've heard different versions of this story again and again. The details vary, but the results are the same: kids who hear negative messages about themselves from adults internalize those perceptions, creating a negative self-image, which informs the choices they make in life. All too often, this leads to detrimental decisions with far-reaching consequences.

I am sure that I've made mistakes and bad judgment calls in my years of teaching, but I'm confident that I did this one thing right:

I never called a kid "bad." I never told a child I hated him or her, and I never said that they wouldn't amount to anything.

Not ever.

Most years, during the first week of school, I'd ask the class to close their eyes and put their heads down. Then I would ask them to raise their hands if they had ever been called bad. Usually over half the class raised their hands including, virtually without exception, every black male in class. I would repeat the same thing for "worthless" and "a problem." Then I would tell the kids my expectation for the year:

"I will get mad at you. I may yell at you, even though I don't think that's a good idea. And I will get frustrated. But I want you to know right now that I care about you even when I'm mad. It's my job to take care of you while you're here and I will never ever call you 'bad.' If any grown-up has called you that before, they were wrong. You might have made a bad decision. You might have done something (or a lot of things) that hurt people. But you are not bad."

They got the message. I know it worked, because on more than one occasion, when I was really, *really* angry at a kid, raising my voice against my better judgment, he or she would say, right to my face, "I know you just yelling at me because you care about me, not because you think I'm bad."

I taught my students a number of important things over the years—math, reading, writing, science, social studies, you name it. But if there's one thing I'm especially proud of, it's that they heard me say I cared about them, and they knew I expected good things from them.

I can only hope that in showing every child that he or she was worth caring about, I set a good example for them to follow in caring about both others and themselves. If this has helped them in life, even just a little, then my teaching career has been a success.

CHAPTER 6

LET'S TALK ABOUT RACE

*"There ain't no white kids.
There's only white teachers."*

—FIRST GRADE STUDENT

Life in a "Post-Racial" Society

I recently heard a radio interview with Elizabeth Eckford, one of the Little Rock Nine, the group who were the first black students at Little Rock Central High School and the object of many protests and threats. I'd known that President Eisenhower invoked the US National Guard to protect those students. What I hadn't realized before the radio interview is that the Arkansas National Guard was first deployed to keep the black students *out* of the school. I can't imagine the experience of going to school and having one set of troops trying to keep you out and another trying to get you in.

Unfortunately, I don't have to imagine what segregated schools are like, even though I was born twenty years after *Brown v. Board of Education*. I worked at one for eight years. Some background about the community and demographics of Oakland will help explain.

On the surface, Oakland looks like a perfect melting pot of diversity: 28 percent black and 34.5 percent white. This is fairly close to one-third black, one-third white, and one-third "other." Balance, equality, and fraternity is the ideal outcome of such a diverse population.

But upon closer inspection, a very different reality emerges.

Oakland is extremely segregated, so much so that it is effectively two different cities: the hills and the flatlands. In the hills, you find white children and a few Asians. The "hills schools" when I was teaching tended to be mostly white, with very few children who speak English as a second language. These schools benefit from greater parental involvement and financial resources, and their test scores show it.

Then you have the flatlands. There, you don't typically find white kids. You do find black, Latino, and Asian kids (mostly Southeast Asian). You also find violence. Homicide victims in Oakland are 77 percent black and 3.2 percent white. In other words, homicide victims in the city are twenty-four times more likely to be black than white, even though black people and white people make up close to the same percentage of the population here. You find terrible air quality in the flatlands as well, because industrial trucks are allowed on I-880 where it cuts through that part of town. In contrast, trucks are banned from I-580, the highway that runs much closer to the hills. Heaven forbid the hills' air should be contaminated.

Generally, the only white people in the flatlands are social workers and teachers. But for the most part they vacate these neighborhoods at night, going home to their houses in the hills and other safer areas, and they often work in these neighborhoods for a limited amount of time. There are white people who live in the flatlands by choice, trying to be part of the community they are serving, but they are the minority. Far more common is the white teacher or social worker who gets priced out of the hills, but doesn't want to live in the flatlands. So they move farther and farther away until the commute is too big of a hardship for them to continue working there.

The bottom line is that there have always been white teachers at East Oakland Elementary, but white children don't attend. In fact, while I taught there, no white kids had attended in anyone's memory.

We may have done away with the fallacious notion of "separate but equal" in education decades ago, but de facto segregation and the inequity it breeds is alive and well today at schools like this one.

The Impact of Segregation

On Martin Luther King, Jr. Day during my first year of teaching, we talked about the Civil Rights Movement, and specifically, about the desegregation of schools. During this discussion, one of the kids looked very confused and said, "But black kids don't go to school with white kids." In her experience, this was true.

Not only were there no white kids at our school, but the classes themselves were often made up of students of a single race. This homogeneity was a side effect (or perhaps the intended effect) of *tracking*, sorting students into different classes based on ability (the college prep track, for example), or by some other means—often the language spoken.

When I started, the school was divided into four tracks. For practicality's sake, given our diverse student body, kids were assigned to tracks based on their specific language requirements. Tracks C and D were the Vietnamese and Spanish language tracks, respectively. Track A was "Other Asian/sheltered[3]" and Track B was "English only" (this was somewhat irreverently referred to as the "black track"; not PC, but true).

The inherent problems in this strategy are hardly unpredictable. After all, wasn't it more than sixty years ago that the US Supreme Court decided that separate wasn't equal? When I pointed out to my first principal that I was uncomfortable with the kids being segregated by race, she protested. "They're not segregated by race," she insisted. "They're segregated by language!"

The end result was that most kids had never been in a classroom with children who looked different from them, and because of the different tracks' in-session schedule, may not even have been in the school at the same time (see chapter 3 for more information about the perils of track scheduling). In my second year of teaching, the kids were more racially mixed. There were still Spanish-language, English-only, and sheltered classes, but at least all the kids went to school together at the same time.

On the first day of school, two third-graders walked in the door at about the same time. One, Mark, was black and the other one, Fernando, was Latino. Mark looked at Fernando and, without saying a word, punched him in the nose—hard. Blood splattered on the floor (a great visual for parents dropping their children off on the first day of third grade), and Fernando burst into tears. As I cleaned up the blood, I asked Mark why he had hit the other boy. His response? "He ain't supposed to be in my class."

I didn't understand. "Why is he not supposed to be in your class?" I asked. "And why does that mean you hit him?"

Mark said, "He's Mexican. Ain't supposed to be no Mexicans in my class."

That was enough provocation for him. This was only one example of racial tension, and there were just as many Mexican and Asian families who asked for black kids to be removed from their classes. The tracking system that I had been arguing against—a new version of "separate but

---

[3] Sheltered classrooms are mainly for English language learners and use specific teaching techniques geared to give students basic comprehension of the material.

equal"—had led to fairly predictable results: a lack of understanding that bred ill will and violence between students of different races.

Light and White Privilege

I thought when I started teaching third grade at East Oakland Elementary that the kids there might have more of a realistic view of different races than the other children I had known and worked with in the past, in mostly white areas. Incidents like the one described above with Mark and Fernando quickly proved this assumption on my part wrong. For instance, after repeatedly being asked if I were black or Mexican, I had a startling conversation with my student Andrew.

Our discussion about race went like this:

> Andrew: Teacher, some kids was talking about you, and they was saying you was white. But I stood up for you and I said no you wasn't, you was black.
>
> Me: You told them I was black?
>
> Andrew: Yeah, I stood up for you.
>
> Me: Do you think I'm black?
>
> Andrew: Yeah, you's black. You's just light skinnded.
>
> Me: Andrew, I'm actually white. Look at my skin color. See how light I am?
>
> Andrew: You's white? You's not light skinnded? [long pause] I'ma have to think about this . . .

Kids don't process race in the same way as adults, and they are still working out which categories people fit in. If they love you, they put you in their group. I had made it into Andrew's group.

Once I started paying attention, I found that the overwhelming feeling among my students was that being light skinned was better than being dark skinned. "Light" was used as a synonym for "pretty" or "good-looking," and "good hair" was hair that was closest in color and texture to Caucasian hair. However, kids on both sides of the spectrum suffered. Black kids who were "too light" were afraid of being called white and were taunted by the same kids who spoke jealously of other kids' "good hair." No matter what their skin color was, it somehow turned into a liability for all of the black kids—at least in terms of how they treated one another.

I once heard one kid say to another, "Your mama left you in the oven too long. You look just like a burnt cookie!"

Only for the other to retort, "Oh yeah? Well you look like a white boy. I bet you ain't even black."

It's not hard to figure why the most of the kids assumed that being whiter is better: white privilege is alive and well.

Over the past several years, I've heard a lot of people talk about how racism is dead. Sometimes they don't say it outright, but they talk about "the bad old days" when schools were legally required to be segregated. Or they talk about how, after Barack Obama was elected to the White House, people should stop "whining" about racism. Or how white people aren't any more likely to be promoted/hired than anyone else, and in fact they think so-called reverse discrimination, with minorities supposedly benefiting from hiring quotas, is usually the norm.

As a white person, it is very easy to take all of these examples for granted. In fact, I was turned off by the term "white privilege" for a long time. My dad was a mechanic and my mom a teacher's aide—we didn't grow up with a lot of money. However, white privilege isn't only about financial resources.

I can rest easy in the fact that my ethnicity is generally held up as the standard of beauty in our society, or even just that Band-Aids, Ace Bandages, and "nude" bras are made in my color and no other skin color (at least so far). I have never been followed around in a store by its employees, and I was treated politely the one time I accidentally shoplifted (I completely forgot to take off the t-shirt I had tried on under a sweater, realized my mistake, and rushed back into the store). I am spoken to respectfully by police officers, even when I am in the wrong. I have driven to wealthy neighborhoods for tutoring and waited in my car when I am early, and no one has ever alerted the police that someone from outside their neighborhood was loitering. However, my black friends and colleagues can't take any of these things for granted—for their experience is all too often radically different.

I can cite many examples of times I've seen my students subject to behavior that seemed to have everything to do with their skin color. For instance, there were all the times that my (mostly black) class lined up to get on BART or AC Transit and the driver yelled, "No room!" and rushed off. That may have happened if the kids were white. But really? Would it? *That often?* I've never had an all-white class, but I've been a passenger with many white classes heading to or from field trips who were much more badly behaved than my class ever was, and no one objected, much less refused them access to city transit.

When I would run errands with non-white coworkers, I would see how they were watched carefully by store employees, while I wasn't. And then there were the cleanliness and repair conditions at my school, which would have been considered and treated as intolerable in a mostly white school. Or the fact that my students were—at age eight—already resigned to the fact that they had to be scared of the police.

Then there was the time I was driving around the housing projects near my school with a black co-worker to do a home visit. This area was known to be unsafe, and it was getting dark. Now, this co-worker had basically the same educational background as me, except that she had gone to a better school. We had the same job, and we were of the same social class.

As we were driving, she pointed out that I was much less likely to get shot than she was. This didn't make a lot of sense to me until she added, "If we both got shot, the police would find out who did it for you. There would be an outcry, and people would demand justice. That wouldn't happen for me."

And she was right. I wouldn't have agreed with her ten years earlier. I understand why others may not agree, and why they want to believe that our society is past that. I understand not wanting to see it, or honestly just *not* seeing it because it's not happening to you.

But if you really disagree that racism is still a problem in the United States, I challenge you to test what you believe. Ask your black friends, coworkers, and family members about these kinds of things. Ask them for their stories. Until you've experienced it or heard that it has happened to someone you know and care about, it's easy to believe these kinds of things don't happen anymore.

And if you're not willing to ask—what does that show?

How to Address Racism

As a teacher, I always strive to help all students—regardless of color, body shape or size, physical ability, or intelligence—to feel accepted for who they are. That desire might be behind my historical tendency to shy away from using racial descriptors.

For example, a friend and I were in a crowded public area when I saw a woman in a really short skirt. I nudged my friend and looked toward the woman, but my friend didn't see her. I whispered to her what I was looking at (the skirt was *really* short) and my friend still didn't see her. I tried a few other descriptors: the woman with short hair, the woman with brown shoes, etc. Then I realized what I didn't say. I didn't say that I was looking at the black woman. That would have identified her right away.

The teachers at East Oakland Elementary generally did their best to pretend that they were colorblind, much as I did with my friend that day. Teachers would engage in verbal gymnastics to avoid any mention of race or color. Instead, we would focus on less obvious characteristics in order to identify a student. We might have mentioned hairstyles, height, or other things that are difficult to see from across a playground, avoiding the topic of race at all costs.

On the surface, a colorblind approach may seem progressive and even enlightened. However, I am reminded of comedian and noted satirist Stephen Colbert. He once said that he doesn't see race, but people tell him he's white and he believes them, because police officers call him "sir."

In many ways, it is easy for me—as a middle-class white woman—to act colorblind, since I am rarely the target of discrimination. Indeed, the fear that I and other white teachers (which make up the vast majority of teachers in the United States, over 82% in 2012)[4] felt about mentioning

---

[4] https://aacte.org/news-room/aacte-in-the-news/347-student-diversity-is-up-but-teachers-are-mostly-white.

race may have been a symptom of our discomfort at acknowledging our white privilege. To a person of color, the act of a white teacher claiming "enlightened colorblindness" may seem more like willfully turning a blind eye to the reality of communities like the flatlands in Oakland. Whether out of naïveté or just the fact that they were not beneficiaries of the entrenched system, the kids did not share the teachers' hang-ups about talking about something as obvious as race.

Day in and out, I heard comments from the kids like, "that white teacher gave me a pencil," "that Mexican kid hit me," or "that black girl is my friend." It felt a little jarring at times, especially in the beginning. But for the most part, the children were using these terms simply as descriptors, not as put-downs. It was often the easiest way to identify someone.

The kids' methods were not always foolproof, of course. There were many incidences of a child announcing that "that Chinese kid" hit him, only for the child in question to vehemently declare that he wasn't Chinese, he was Cambodian, and never to call him Chinese again. In addition, there were times when the descriptor had so much disrespect in the tone that you could tell the child was using "black" or "white" as a way to say something much worse. Almost any word can feel like a racial slur when said with enough disgust. However, much of the time, the kids were honestly just trying to use the simplest way to describe a classmate.

I discovered a unique way to get my students and myself more comfortable with talking about race and color while leaving the baggage of stereotypes and racism behind.

One day I brought a large envelope full of paint chips, with all the names of the colors blacked out. I had chosen every feasible skin tone, from almost pure white to deep black, and every shade of red, yellow, and brown in between. The students were first tasked with each finding their own skin tone. At first we had some tears, along with comments like, "I don't want to be this color, I want to be that one." There were also kids who were very unrealistic and picked colors much lighter than their actual skin tone, just out of wishful thinking. Eventually, everyone seemed to find their own color, although I was glad when kids began to get creative and figure out that they weren't one solid color. They found colors for their face and their legs and the palms of their hands. For once, not a single child belittled another during this project. They were too caught up in their own self-discovery.

Next, they got to name their color. They cut out the paint chip (or chips) they had chosen and glued them onto a piece of paper with a caption. Chocolate was a common theme, as everyone who had brown skin seemed to want to name their color after a type of chocolate. Peach was also common, with "peach milkshake" being chosen for me. One child decided he was the color of "peanut butter power." Again, not a single student offered up a derogatory name for anyone else's color.

I think the reason why this activity worked is because it tapped into the kids' creativity. The name-calling came back eventually, of course, but at least for that day everyone seemed to be proud to be who they were and proud of the color of their own skin. I hope that's something all of them were able to carry with them, if and when they needed it.

While the paint chip exercise was a useful springboard to meaning-ful, positive discussion, I can't claim that I've always handled talking about race perfectly. Clearly, I have my own issues and biases around it, as we all do. But I found that when students asked me questions and I answered directly, they were happy to get an answer. Kids are naturally curious and wanted to know why my skin didn't look like theirs. And they're not afraid to keep asking questions—about everything from why I get sunburned so fast, to if I had any black friends growing up.

This can be a frightening conversation to have, even for a teacher. Race is an extremely emotionally charged subject and, as a white teacher who once taught a class entirely made up of students of color, I was often afraid that my comments would be seen as insensitive or taken out of context. However, I've learned that children understand when people are being genuine. And an honest conversation is an excellent starting point to create a dialogue that leads to greater understanding. Maybe we can all just take the direct approach more often and accept ourselves and each other as we are, without stereotypes or misplaced colorblindness—peach milkshake, peanut butter power, and all.

CHAPTER 7:

TEACHING TO TRAUMA

"You can't patch a wounded soul with a Band-Aid."

—MICHAEL CONNELLY,
The Black Echo

Our Nation's Youngest Walking Wounded

The kids of East Oakland Elementary were no strangers to trauma, and the sources of this were as heartbreaking as they were varied. Most had seen someone killed at some point—whether a neighbor, friend, or relative. Most also had a family member incarcerated, usually for drugs, or sometimes for armed robbery, assault, or even murder or attempted murder. Bottom line: violence, abuse, neglect, and crime were a common part of life for these kids, but that doesn't mean they were any more immune to the effects of trauma than children living in safer neighborhoods.

On the contrary, they very much needed help to deal with the after effects of trauma, PTSD, and other emotional and mental health issues that resulted from or were exacerbated by their life circumstances. And as their teacher, again and again I saw our educational and healthcare systems fail to provide this much-needed care.

One of my students, a third grader, saw her grown cousin shot in the face and still came to school the next day. She didn't stop shaking all week. That year was one of many when our school had no counseling resources. This student's whole family was overwhelmed with grief and lacked the finances to take her to counseling. I didn't know what to do. I talked to her when she wanted and left her alone when she wanted, but I was completely in over my head.

Another child saw her father get shot in the head when she was six years old, the result of a drug deal gone bad. She failed first grade after falling far behind due to many absences when her mother could not bring her to school, having trouble simply getting out of bed, and the child's own inability to learn, both clearly due to trauma. A few years later, while in my third-grade class, she was triggered to the point of being unable to stay in the room when we read a story about a father because she was hyperventilating. Once I changed the lesson plan slightly because the story we were reading featured a father, and I knew that would be a trigger for her. I was reprimanded by the reading coach, in front of the students. The coach said I should just send anyone having a problem out of the classroom. Sending her out wasn't the nurturing approach that this student needed.

Dealing with the effects of extreme violence and trauma on children was never officially in my job description, and yet it was a part of my everyday experience as a teacher at East Oakland Elementary.

Even after teaching there for years, it's hard for me to imagine children having to deal with these kinds of issues. How can anyone be expected to teach anything in a setting where nearly every day a child in the class is processing these kinds of horrors? Worse, when my administrators observed me trying to help a traumatized child, they often reprimanded me for taking time away from teaching to the lesson plan, and as a result, "failing in my duty to help our students meet their academic standards."

I lacked the freedom to change the scheduled topic to deal with these situations as they came up. I couldn't take class time to talk about the children's feelings about what was going on.

In cases where I saw clear signs of abuse or neglect, I was obligated to call Social Services. While they may have been better equipped to deal with the situation, it still often ended badly for the child; he or she usually ended up getting hit at home for telling other people their family business. One child got a visit from a social worker at home after one of my calls. He told me he could never talk to me about anything again because he had gotten in trouble. I found a note later on the floor that said, "Ms. Harris, now you can't help me, now nobody can help me."

I only personally saw Child Protective Services step in once. A child had told me that his mother's boyfriend wanted the two of them to move away and leave the kids. When the mother balked at this, the boyfriend made a horrifically violent threat against the children—in front of them—telling them and their mother in graphic detail what he would do to them if she refused to abandon them. I confirmed this threat with the mother and called the authorities immediately. I assume CPS had received other calls about this family because they came that day and interviewed the child at school, which I hadn't personally seen before. The next week, that boy's uncle showed up to talk to me.

I will never forget this man.

He told me that he didn't have children of his own and didn't really know how to raise kids, but that he had been granted custody of his nephew (my student) and niece. He said he loved them and would do his best. We both cried. What else could we do, in a situation like that?

Given the extraordinary conditions that our students were facing day in and day out, it's not surprising that we were what the government and many others call a "failing" school. It didn't matter if my students were suffering from malnutrition, fetal alcohol syndrome, neglect, abuse, or PTSD, or if—on top of all of that—they didn't speak English or their parents were illiterate. I needed to be sure that they learned their parts of speech quickly or the government would impose sanctions (taking away instructional assistants or field trip funding, for example) or even close our school.

While I worked at this school, I learned firsthand, over and over again, the tragic results of our educational system's inability to recognize—let alone support—the needs of entire communities of children suffering from the effects of trauma.

Shawna's Story: Struggle and a Reason to Hope

When I talked about my classroom to teacher friends at other schools I usually referred to my class as a special day class (SDC), a code they would understand for explaining that I had a class full of emotionally disturbed children, as many of my twenty students were highly needy in this regard. Technically, a special day class was a small, specialized classroom of students with different needs and diagnoses, taught by a teacher who is trained for this situation. Although my students had many characteristics of those attending SDCs, my class was not officially classified as such, and therefore, I had none of the support, benefits, training, or reduced class size that accompanies the designation.

Shawna's classification as SED (severely emotionally disturbed), would have normally qualified her for special day classes. But because there was no room in the appropriate classes (and none offered on our campus), she was placed in my mainstream class. She usually presented as a very sweet girl with severe learning problems, who often talked about how much she loved me, her family, and her bunny. At the same time, Shawna had extreme anger issues when she became frustrated.

We worked on using words to express her frustration, but meltdowns were frequent. And I mean *meltdowns*. For example, if she couldn't understand something, she would pull *every* single one of the four hundred books in the classroom off the bookshelves and throw them across the room, rip posters off the wall and tear them in half, knock over desks, and try to stab people with scissors.

When a meltdown happened, the rest of the day was shot—not just for her, but for everyone. It was hard for the other children—or even me and any other adults helping out that day—to recover after witnessing or being the target of these violent outbursts. The other children were so shocked from watching that they usually weren't able to focus. Regaining their attention was practically impossible, since Shawna's meltdowns put the room in such disarray that it was hard to continue the lesson plans, as by then, class materials were strewn all over the room. Several times I had to take the kids out to play while an administrator put things away.

Shawna had experienced traumatic abuse when she was an infant. The abuser, her biological father, was in prison and no longer in her life. She and her twin sister (who had not been abused) were being raised by her mother and a loving stepfather. Her behavior was so extreme that I had a meeting with her parents and our principal very quickly and, since they were in complete agreement about Shawna needing a different environment, called in the district special education specialist, who sent a social worker to observe Shawna.

It's worth noting that the social worker who decided Shawna needed help saw her on a *good* day, when she destroyed none of my property and didn't physically hurt any other children. The social worker did see, though, how easily Shawna spiraled down into frustration and self-hatred, how far behind she was academically, and how she seemed to emotionally regress quickly, requiring significant redirection.

Before meeting with Shawna's parents again, the head of special education and my principal told me that we would be asked some questions at the upcoming meeting—specifically, if we thought that Shawna's emotional problems led to her acting out and her problems with learning. The two of them had talked before and the principal told me that our only option was to answer no to this question, that we thought these things were totally unrelated. I disagreed and told her so. She responded with something about "district services" and told me again to simply answer "no."

I later learned that if disruptive behavior was caused by a student's diagnosis, the school district is required to provide adequate services (in Shawna's case, expensive ones) for the student. But if they could make the case that the child's emotional problems were not a factor in her behavior in class and that the child *was* "responsible" for that behavior, "we" could just blame the parents and move on.

The—at best—questionable ethics of being instructed to speak against what I knew to be true as Shawna's teacher infuriated me. A child who desperately needed additional services finally had a shot at getting them. But instead of doing the right thing and supporting this child and her teacher, the administrators pressured us to lie so that the district could save money.

I met with Shawna's parents, my principal, and the head of special education, who quickly proved herself to be rude, condescending, overbearing, and elitist. She blamed Shawna's mother, who sobbed through the whole meeting. This mother was one of the few parents I met while teaching at East Oakland Elementary who took responsibility for her emotionally disturbed child (a hard thing for any parent) and didn't just deny that there was a problem. She said that she'd been wanting help for her daughter for years, and she just didn't know how to go about getting it.

When it came time for the questions, the principal said that no, she did not think that Shawna's emotional problems were related to her problems at school. The administrator wrote that down and turned to me. I said that I disagreed and that I thought her problems at school had *everything* to do with her emotional problems and her diagnoses. I was asked to restate that. I did.

Everyone looked at me and the principal disagreed with me, even though she was on my side before speaking with the head of special education. So I restated my position yet again. The special education administrator dealt with this by snapping at Shawna's mother, calling her parenting into question. At that point, Shawna's mother became so upset she had to leave the room. I was reprimanded for what I'd said, but since I already had tenure, I couldn't be fired. Still, this is one of those situations that I *really* wished I had recorded.

Ultimately, Shawna was placed in the counseling-enriched small special day class where she needed to be and where she had a full-time aide. Since then, that particular special education administrator is no longer with the district, the principal has changed schools, and I have left the classroom. Shawna got help, though. Her sister came to visit me quite often, with reports of how much happier Shawna was in her new class. I also received some notes from Shawna that indicated she was doing better. Her new teacher had helped her to write them, another clear sign that Shawna was finally receiving the one-on-one attention and care she needed in order to heal and learn.

I was and still am hopeful for her future.

Another Child Slips through the Cracks

That same year another student in my third-grade class, Jennie, had forty-five absences and many tardies at the halfway point of the school year. Her mother always excused them, explaining that Jennie had been throwing up or having diarrhea. Jennie's brother had almost as many absences; the word was that he too was the victim of frequent stomach upsets.

For a variety of reasons, I suspected Jennie's father of being violent and abusive toward Jennie's mother and probably also toward the children. My teacher's instinct said that the extreme gastrointestinal distress exhibited by Jennie and her brother, as well as their guarded, almost silent demeanor, might be a direct result of the tension in their home.

I put in the paperwork for an attendance board review for Jennie, and nothing ever came of it. When I followed up with the principal and assistant principal, they had me resubmit the paperwork, and still, nothing was done.

No review board, no investigation, no action whatsoever.

Jennie's behavior was not a problem at school and she wasn't too far behind grade level, so nobody at the administrative level was overly concerned about her, even though her frequent illnesses were a strong signal that something was wrong. By the end of the school year, she had missed almost half of the school days that year, and I was told to just pass her on to fourth grade because "no one has time to deal with it."

All of the teachers who had ever dealt with Jennie's family agreed that there were many signs of abuse, from the mother's fear of displeasing her husband, to the kids' nervousness and stomach problems, to how they avoided talking about home or their father. But because these kids weren't "behavior problems," their obvious distress was ignored.

Those kids and their mother likely needed help. If we'd only had a school counselor or social workers available to heed the warnings that I and Jennie's other teachers gave, things might have been different for the family. It breaks my heart.

Feelings on Paper

Difficult emotions can be frightening for all of us, especially children. But if students don't have the vocabulary to express those feelings, they often turn to acting out. This response doesn't help the student because it fails to resolve the difficult feelings and makes a teacher's job much more difficult.

In order to coach my students to a more productive response to their often overwhelming emotions, I learned to focus on the reason behind the behavior. Everyone responds differently to situations or feelings. Some children hit others when they become angry or frustrated. Others talk incessantly when they are nervous or excited. Still others stop responding completely when they are sad, or may even show signs of self-harm. Students often can't see that these feelings and behaviors are connected. As teachers, we can and must help students voice their feelings.

One of my proudest achievements in my teaching career was creating a tool for helping children express their emotions. I had seen some magnets and posters that had pictures of different facial expressions with the names of the corresponding emotions underneath. I took this idea and picked out the emotions most applicable for my students. I created slips of paper with the phrase "I feel" followed by a variety of emotions they could check: angry, sad, disappointed, worried, frustrated, nervous, excited, happy, and more. There was also a space for their names and notes for further explanation. I included one more option at the bottom: "I just need attention."

I explained my ground rules to the kids. The papers would be kept in a corner of the room and they could get up to take one at any point—as long as they were quiet. They could fill these out, no matter what else we were doing in class, and hand it to me or put it on my desk. I explained that I may not be able to look at it right away, and that even if I did, there was no guarantee that I could do something right away, but as soon as I could, I would talk to them about it.

The kids *never* misused this tool. I found my students very often didn't need me to do anything. Many of them truly just needed to acknowledge—and for someone else to acknowledge—what they were feeling, or as I had predicted, they just needed some attention.

Some words had to be explained, of course. "Frustrated" was an exceptionally powerful word for many children who had never known what it was that made them feel like hitting something or breaking their pencil. A common write-in was that the writer wanted to hit someone, so we had a class discussion (and many, many individual discussions) about how it was acceptable to *feel like* hitting someone, as long as you didn't *actually* hit someone. I knew I was getting through when one particularly troubled girl ran toward my desk, fists clenched, saying, "I'm not going to do it, but I want to hit her. So I'm telling you instead."

My students also learned that it's possible to have many emotions at the same time, and this paper helped them sort all those feelings out. One boy, whose mom was getting out of jail soon, kept taking the papers and filling them out with "happy," "excited," and "nervous" all checked. He didn't want anything from me—he just wanted to keep saying it. Another child checked every single emotion, every time. His life was a tornado of emotions, and he often added that he hated himself. Seeing that he needed extra attention, I made it a point to take the time to talk to him at recess on a regular basis.

Another girl filled out a "feelings paper," as the students called them, almost every day, and checked "I just need attention" every time. She would then underline it multiple times, circle it, and add exclamation marks. Sometime she would rewrite it several times. The amazing part was that she really did just need attention. I would get one of these papers in my hand, walk over to her, comment on her work, touch her shoulder, or just say hi, and she'd be all right for a little while.

Some kids were less able to cope with feelings than others. These students would alternate between crying, raging, and blaming themselves. I learned to sit with them when I could and say, "It's okay. You're okay right now. I know you feel bad but you're okay and we're going to do this together." Those words were all I had to dole out to kids who had seen some horrible things, or had people leave them who shouldn't have left them, or who just *hated* themselves. At those times, all I could do was to hug them and say "You're okay. I'm taking care of you right now, and you're okay." I think the most I could give them was a feeling of being all right, just for that one minute. It was inadequate but I hope it was better than nothing.

These papers didn't solve any of the problems in my students' lives. They still had parents who were incarcerated, still witnessed and suffered abuse, and still experienced the tragedies that come with living in a low-income, high-violence area. But the act of identifying their feelings and having them validated was a tool that helped them take control over their emotions. As a result, they were less at the mercy of their feelings and more able to determine what they needed. At the very least, my goal was that, as they got older, they would remember that their feelings are always valid, and that someone along the way cared about helping them figure that out.

Resilience Is an Excuse, Not a Strategy

While I taught at East Oakland Elementary, many of my students—as many as 75 percent of my class many years—displayed symptoms of post-traumatic stress disorder (PTSD). At one point, I found myself in a teachers' workshop where the presenters proclaimed that kids are resilient and simply need supportive people in their lives in order to succeed.

I wanted to tell them, "Come look in the eyes of kids who live in neighborhoods like East Oakland and see how much resilience they have left."

When it comes to kids, resilience is a tricky concept. There is truth to it—children do survive some of the most atrocious situations that I could imagine and often seem to recover quickly from illness, abuse, and loss. But I think relying on their resilience is dangerous. Well-intentioned people like those presenters throw around statements like, "Oh, kids are resilient. He'll be fine." But in so many cases that I saw as a teacher, my students were not *recovering* from these situations as much as they were simply *surviving* them. And, no, they were not fine.

We must differentiate this crucial nuance.

Kids who survive trauma without the aid of counseling and other much-needed services are not thriving, nor are they growing or succeeding as they should. In cases like these, children's resilience shouldn't be used as an excuse for not taking action. Kids knowing how to survive should not excuse us from doing everything in our power to help them recover from life-altering trauma.

We recognize the need to treat PTSD in our returning troops; surely we should offer the same for our youth who experience traumatic stress in their own neighborhoods. We also can and should work to offer safer conditions, so we can pre-empt rather than have to treat conditions like PTSD in the first place.

CHAPTER 8

ENDING THE CYCLE OF POVERTY

"*Poverty is the worst form of violence.*"

—MAHATMA GANDHI

The Slow Death of the American Dream

There's another experience of trauma, beyond witnessing violence or the victimization of loved ones—one that also removes any hope of a sense of safety and security from childhood: extreme poverty. Every one of my students lived this reality every day.

In spite of our idea of the American Dream, it's harder than ever to move up on the socioeconomic ladder here, and hard work is no longer enough to lift most people out of poverty. A Pew Research report[5] shows that the likelihood of a person who was born into a specific quintile[6] of overall wealth distribution in the United States moving up during their lifetime. In a phenomenon they call "stuck at the ends," very few people in the bottom quintile are able to get to the next level, and the people at the top tend to stay there. People at the bottom of the socioeconomic scale find that, most months, unexpected expenses prevent them from saving any money. Half of black, single parents without a college education have less than $75 of savings that they have immediate access to[7], meaning that they're not living week to week or paycheck to paycheck but rather day to day. In that situation, even a minor financial problem becomes a major catastrophe.

In the United States, education has always been seen as the most likely way for people to escape poverty, and historically this has tended to be true. However, this has changed for Americans with the least resources. First, more jobs now require higher levels of education. Second, more disadvantaged schools are producing less capable students because of the lack of educational opportunities provided, which is beyond the students' control. This means some type of post-high school education is often needed to gain skills and knowledge that are no longer part of a high school education. However, this is not universal; schools are becoming more segregated again, with top schools improving, while

---

[5] http://www.pewtrusts.org/en/multimedia/video/2011/economic-mobility-and-the-american-dream

[6] A quintile is one of any of five equal groups into which a population can be divided according to the distribution of values of a particular variable.

[7] http://www.pewtrusts.org/en/multimedia/data-visualizations/2016/portrait-of-financial-security

mostly urban, majority-minority schools stagnate or even deteriorate. These majority-minority schools are also more frequently subject to experimentation with charter or for-profit systems, reducing the money going into traditional classrooms even more.

Fundamentally, America's decision to fund public education at the local level reinforces the "rich get richer" dynamic: schools in top districts are in pricy neighborhoods, where higher property taxes result in more resources for the local school. Additionally, the families who can afford to live in these neighborhoods are more likely to have the money for tutors, music lessons, summer camps, and other educational activities. Even within Oakland, schools have radically different amounts of resources, because some schools' PTAs can raise enormous amounts of money.

And in the midst of all of this, the social safety net has been significantly weakened in the last few decades. Food stamps and other assistance programs have been cut in many areas, and many jobs have been outsourced, making it harder to find employment. At the same time, costs faced by people of limited means, such as medical expenses, have grown at a faster pace than the rest of the economy.

Thinking about all this, it's not hard to see how the promise of the American Dream, which has been such an important part of our nation's identity, is failing today's low-income families, trapping multiple generations in a cycle of crushing poverty.

Growing Up Poor in America

The reality of the circumstances described above for me as a teacher was that many of the low-income kids in my class regularly came to school not only hungry, but physically and emotionally exhausted. Difficult financial straits meant that they weren't getting enough rest or enough to eat, and as I've described in other chapters, they were under a level of stress that children in higher income brackets usually never know until they reach adulthood—if ever at all. All of this had a significant effect on my students' attention and ability to learn in school.

In addition to simply not having the money for food, or for nutritious food, whatever parents or guardians my students were living with often worked long or odd hours out of necessity, leaving the children without adequate adult supervision at home. Oldest siblings often cared not only for themselves, but also for their younger brothers and sisters. In some cases, these students were the *de facto* head of household for the whole day from the time that they were in kindergarten.

I had one student in my first grade class named David. David was very small, even for a first grader. When I saw him set out walking home from school alone one day, I asked him if his mom was all right with that, or if he should wait for an older friend or cousin. He said, "My mama says I'm grown now and I have to act grown."

At that moment, I didn't realize the full meaning of that pronouncement. Over time, I learned more about his family situation. David was the oldest child, with a younger brother and baby sister at home. His mother worked incessantly at low-wage jobs to provide for her family, often at all hours.

During the long hours that she was away, David was essentially the head of the household. He was in charge of getting breakfast ready, giving the baby her bottle, getting everyone dressed, and getting himself and his younger brother to school and the baby to a neighbor's house if his mom was still not home. Out of necessity, this tiny six-year-old was considered an adult with adult responsibilities.

David was often hungry himself, which was no surprise, given that he was trying to run a household without the knowledge and tools required to do so. Exhausted by his responsibilities at home, he frequently fell asleep in class and was unable to focus because he hadn't eaten. He also showed clear signs of neglect. One day I had to send him home because his mouth was bleeding so badly from an infection. He said his tooth had been hurting for a long time but his mom "didn't know what to do about it." I gave her referrals to free dentists and she didn't take him. His mouth just kept bleeding for the rest of the week; eventually, I had to make a report of neglect to Child Protective Services.

How can a child feel safe and secure when he can't get his basic medical needs taken care of? Or when at *six years old*, he is the caretaker for his family?

At the same time, as a low-income single parent who lacked much-needed resources and support, the kind of choice David's mother had to make—getting in enough work hours to keep her kids fed, clothed, and off the street, or taking time off work to take them to the doctor or dentist when needed—is heartbreakingly common.

As a society, we need to do better by families like David's.

Nutrition in East Oakland Elementary

David was not the only hungry student in my class. Many of my students did not eat breakfast before arriving at school in the morning. In some cases, their parents didn't have money for food. In others, a child's hunger was due to neglect. And in still other cases, the lone parent in a single-parent household was so overwhelmed that he or she couldn't possibly get everything together in the morning, or even get the child there in time for the free breakfast provided by the school.

Occasionally, my students hadn't eaten dinner the night before either. Hunger was a common cause of behavioral problems in class. Gradually, I taught the hungry kids to use their words and tell me what was wrong instead of just acting out. A lot of the time, a granola bar made the difference in how their day went.

Even this solution proved complicated, however. Other kids would see me giving out a snack, and then they would want some too. I couldn't afford to feed breakfast to twenty kids every day, not to mention all my former students who habitually went hungry and still came back to me for food. I knew which ones had been fending for themselves and who probably hadn't eaten since dinner the night before, or even since the previous day's school lunch. So I ended up having to triage the kids—who did I think was the hungriest? And who seemed most out of control?

I had to balance how much food I had and how the rest of the kids would react to certain children getting to eat. Research shows over and over that if children (or adults) don't have their basic needs met, they can't learn. And teachers want their students to learn. So we keep buying granola bars.

My students were acutely aware that they had less than other kids. When we went on field trips, they would ask me, "Is this where the rich people live? These houses look like rich people houses." They would often point out that white people in the grocery stores buy more food than their family was able to, and that other people didn't have to live where there was shooting most nights.

As I've moved on to private tutoring, not surprisingly, I've been working with students whose families are much better off financially than the families of my former students. I've noticed that, in general, these more privileged kids are not aware of how fortunate they are. At one point, a student who went to a very good public middle school in a wealthy area asked me why so many people eat at McDonald's. Her family was big on whole grains, vegetables, and homemade soups, and she thought that eating at McDonald's was gross. "Why would people feed that stuff to their children?" she asked.

I told her that I agreed and tried to explain the concept of a food desert— how some people don't have grocery stores in their neighborhoods, don't have cars to get to a store, and don't have enough money to buy that kind of food—so the dollar menu might end up looking pretty attractive when their kids are hungry.

She's a smart girl, and she got it. She had just never realized this before and asked me a few times if I was sure there were neighborhoods without grocery stores. I described the neighborhood where I had taught and told her that a lot of the families were only able to shop at liquor stores. She took it all in and said, "I wish there was a way we could get good food to them."

Amen, sister.

Learning How to Eat

Nutrition education was another privilege unique to the more affluent areas. Though the children I tutored from the Oakland and Berkeley hills took cooking classes at school and learned about nutrition and health, the students I taught in the flatlands had no such opportunity. Their ignorance was evident in comments that would have been humorous if they weren't so sad. Knowing that many of my students' parents had had similar educational experiences as my students, I should not have been surprised that misinformation was passed down from generation to generation.

During one field trip, I heard a mother tell her daughter, "Drink your orange soda before you eat your Twinkie. It's your fruit." She really meant well–she was trying to keep her daughter healthy. But she honestly didn't know that soda was not fruit, no matter what artificial flavor was in it. Another student told her friend that she was only drinking Sprite and Sierra Mist from now on because they were healthy, not like Coke and Pepsi. Their families just literally did not have the knowledge that soda was not a healthy choice. They wanted to do the best for their children, but they were not equipped, and educators were not helping by only teaching to the test rather than in a holistic way when it came to health topics. (I've already described in other chapters—at some length—the resistance I encountered from the administration on those occasions I tried to tweak the curriculum to better suit the needs of students in this particular community.)

Another student once asked a colleague of mine if she had brought "white people food" for lunch. It turned out that this student meant salad. Before judging these families for being unhealthy, consider that the only place for them to buy food nearby was the corner liquor store. A shopping trip to a store that provided healthier options would probably involve hand-carrying the groceries on a bus (or several buses) with children tagging along, because childcare was not available. Many parents worked such long hours at low-wage jobs that even the time it would take to get to a real grocery store was in short supply. As a result, fresh produce was not usually an option.

Bottom line, when you're living on the edge of homelessness in an urban food desert, eating healthy is a luxury. Fast-food dollar items become a simple matter of expediency because they are an affordable way to ensure your child feels full instead of hungry. In this situation, it's almost impossible to think past the immediate crisis of not having enough to eat.

Although they often had the details completely wrong, the children understood conceptually that nutrition was important to good health, as shown by the career aspirations of Ruby:

> My dream is to be a pediatrician because I want kids to be safe and have a better Life and have someone who cares about them.

The reason I want to be a peditairican so I can help kids so They can be smart in school what I like about a pediatricain that I get to help small children and be heathly because some kids can die because the don't eat fruit and stuff so they won't be so sick and I want chidlen to Live heathly Lives like we do we want children to Live as Long as us.

Unfortunately, the gap between "knowing" and "doing" was cavernous. Ruby routinely ate Flamin' Hot Cheetos with nacho "cheese" and a Pepsi for breakfast right before the bell rang. Future physician, heal thyself! But to do that would require knowledge of and access to healthy food.

Esteban, Aspiring Gang Leader

Another common element of poverty-stricken neighborhoods is the presence of gangs. There are many reasons for this, of course, but one big one is the need to belong and to feel like there are people who have your back—who will take care of you. You can see that children like David, in charge of his entire family at age six, would be absolutely craving this kind of perceived stability and be ready to join the first group that offered it.

It was unnerving to see one of my former students, Esteban, start a gang. It was all the more so because he was only in fourth grade at the time, but he knew what he was doing, recruiting kids who needed to belong or be noticed. We're not just talking about a "No Girlz Allowed" clique meeting in a treehouse. He would go around to other kids and say things like "That's a nice coat. You want to keep that coat, you'll have to give me three dollars every day." It was small then—if mean-spirited—but I could see exactly where Esteban might end up if he kept going down this path, and it made me terribly afraid for him.

It may have been unnerving, but it wasn't particularly surprising that Esteban was getting sucked into a cycle of violence. He had a number of risk factors, including:

1. He had been out of school for two years because his mom didn't have her life together enough to enroll him.
2. His mom was working as a prostitute.

3. His mom had substance abuse problems.
4. His mom was in very obviously abusive relationships. (Every time I saw her, she had a new black eye or a tooth knocked out.)
5. Off and on, Esteban was being raised by his disabled grandmother who "couldn't handle him" and told him so frequently.
6. His dad was in and out of his life, as he was on and off drugs.
7. And finally, Esteban had been the victim of a variety of forms of abuse.

This list, taken as a whole, is a textbook example of reasons why people join gangs. Kids who are trapped in a cycle of poverty and violence long for a sense of belonging and safety that is absent from their life circumstances. Even children who swear they will never get involved with gangs when they are young find themselves needing support as they get older, and if they can't get it from family or school, a gang may begin to look like a very appealing option.

In Esteban's case, these forces combined to turn him into a mean-spirited, manipulative, cynical bully—by age ten. As the leader of the gang, he received the added respect of his followers.

Underneath his tough exterior, I saw a little of Esteban's true heart on a field trip. We were at the Lawrence Hall of Science observing some animals, including a dove, a snake, a bearded dragon lizard, a chinchilla, and a big rat. None of the kids wanted to go near the rat. After all, we had plenty of rats in East Oakland, and everyone agreed that they were "nasty." But this child—this big, mean, dirty child whom no one liked and who was mean to everyone—he worried that the rat would suffer from hurt feelings because no one wanted anything to do with it.

So he stood by the rat for an hour, talking to it, and telling me periodically that he thought the rat had probably taken a bath, so people should not say that it smelled, that it probably just needed attention. For that hour, he cared for that animal like he was its mother. Esteban was showing the rat the kind of love and security that he himself needed and wasn't getting.

The rat didn't need this reassurance. Esteban did.

It's not hard to see why he started a gang. And if statistics are to be believed, he'll continue to go down that road until he's locked up or dead. It hurts my heart to even write that, but statistically those are the most likely outcomes for kids who join and stay in gangs.

By the way, the average life expectancy for gang members? Twenty years and five months[8]. The average kid who joins a gang doesn't even make it to age twenty-one.

How the Other Half Lives

During my years as a teacher, I learned how my students viewed people with more money. But as I segued into private tutoring, I began to see how surprised upper-middle class and upper-class students were to find out that there were children their age living in poverty in the same city as them.

One private school student I tutored, upon learning I volunteered as a Big Sister for a girl close to her age, peppered me with questions. My answers only led to still more questions. Why did kids like my Little Sister need people to volunteer to spend time with them? Did they all have only one parent? What did it feel like to have one parent in jail? Do kids with parents in jail know why their parents are in jail? Do they think their parents are good people even if they're in jail?

What did I mean some parents don't have cars? How do they get their kids to appointments? Don't they get to go on vacation? Some people don't make enough money to go on vacation? What do they do if they need help in school and can't afford a tutor? What if they need to go to the hospital and they don't have a car? So, the things I did with my Little Sister were just things that she (my tutoring student) did with her own parents? Why did I spend time with this girl when I was so busy?

She ended with: "Can you write down the website for this program? I think I'd like to learn more about it."

It astounded me that none of these kids had any idea about how people in other economic situations live, or even that there *is* another way to live. These weren't celebrity children. None of them lived in a gated compound. They had just never been around children born into poverty.

---

[8] http://www.nwitimes.com/news/gang-members-on-path-of-assumed-destiny-dying-by-age/article_a9110339-5381-56dc-af4c-8d1224a162a9.html

They could easily spend their whole lives having no idea that there were people less than two miles away struggling to get enough food.

The kids in the low-income neighborhoods, on the other hand, are all too aware that there is an "other half." The students may have many misconceptions about people in a higher socioeconomic class (that all white people have big houses and don't have to work, for example), but my students knew that these people existed.

I am reluctant to write about Esteban's trajectory as a teenager because I'm afraid it will feed stereotypes and increase fear of people from neighborhoods like East Oakland—especially teenagers and young adults. But this is what I want people to understand: people from backgrounds like my students, who grow up to be mean, started as wonderful children. They came into this world full of creativity, love, and innocence. But in the cases of some of my students, the intense suffering they endure—nearly all of which can be tied directly back to the cycle of poverty—beats the kindness out of them.

We have to figure out a way to break this cycle—preferably while kids are young—before hopelessness, bitterness, and cruelty have a chance to set in. I believe the answer is more caring adults. I realize this sounds simplistic, but the cycle I see over and over is that kids act out because they believe there is no other way to survive.

We need to realize that home life is an essential part of school. Constant insecurity takes its toll on any of us, whether you are literally living in a war zone or chronically homeless. A clinician in Portland, Oregon stated that children are much more at risk of suffering PTSD, anxiety, and depression when they live with financial insecurity[9]. So we should hardly be surprised that children on the dramatically lower end of the financial insecurity spectrum are having trouble learning. They're more concerned—and rightfully so—with how they are going to simply survive from day to day than with learning their multiplication tables.

There are so many changes that need to be put into effect if we want to help children living in poverty. Feeding them should not be

---

[9] http://www.huffingtonpost.com/2012/05/15/children-mental-health_n_1514845.html

controversial, but every few years, some politician or another wants to take free school lunches off the table or cut food stamp programs dramatically.

The cliché is true: These children are our future. So our choices are simple. We can continue to invest in prisons, or we can instead use that money to dramatically expand low-income housing, work training, and medical (including mental health) services to low-income parents, including undocumented immigrants, whose emotional and financial strain and lack of knowledge has a hugely detrimental effect on their children. In short, we can choose to focus on proactive solutions that uplift people and allow them to live happier, healthier, and more productive lives.

And even putting altruism aside, isn't spending time, energy, and money to combat poverty itself preferable to continuing to expend even more resources needed to deal with its societal consequences? It's past time to break this cycle instead of continuing to feed it.

CHAPTER 9

IN THEIR OWN WORDS

"I learned that people in Africa wear clothes."

—THIRD GRADER,
reflecting on a guest speaker from Africa

My Neighborhood

Kids like my former students are American children living on American soil—in poverty and in a perpetual war zone. If you've never met them, it's disturbingly easy to dismiss these children simply as victims, tragic statistics, or thugs in the making, but they're not; they're just kids. They're silly and smart, funny, and sometimes extremely thoughtful, like any other kids living in any other neighborhood.

Over the years, I've noticed that it is very hard for people who hear these stories to keep in mind that the people in the stories are real children. Knowing the whole child is the only way to truly understand their stories. I've included this chapter to help you know them a little better in their own words, through written work they produced over the years in my class. The writing varies according to how much editing and polishing we did in class.

Every time February rolled around, the third graders as part of the curriculum had to write a little essay about their neighborhood. The students were expected to use sensory details to draw in the audience—a simple enough exercise for many children. But for these kids, the sensory details they included sometimes shocked or scared me or just made me unspeakably sad. Here are some of the essays from the 2006 school year (unedited), from the kids' own first drafts.

Deja:
I here guns popping at night. I here babys crying at night. There little girls outside at night time. Little girls getting raped. I here dogs geting kilt. I here that man geting shot in the back.

Steven:
My neiborhood smells like smoke, food, and musty armpits. It looks messy, juicy, and dirty. It looks nasty, old, and clean. My neiborhood sounds like gun shots, people yelling and babie crying. It smells like acahol [alcohol]. My neiborhood smells like cigerits [cigarettes] and gas from everyone's cars. My neiborhood sounds like people driving and it sound like rain dropping. My neiborhood sounds like people smoking.

Amani:

This is my neighborhood. People are not very nice. Out by my neighborhood. Boys and girls are getting raped at night. It smells like nasty liquid. I have a neighboor next door, and a huge backyard. It looks nasty because it has bottols an food in the sidewalks are in the streets. I hear guns, fights, car acsidents, barking dog, chrildren. The nebiorhood is not so clean because people dont clean up after their selfs. People usally around my house are getto. When my mom walk out of the house there are a lot of thugs on crack. People are crazy and my house is not really quiet.

Jade:

Loud guns and dogs. Clean homes. People and homeys. Smells like food and sausages and smoke. It is dirty sometimes it is quiet sometimes. Their is a lot of trees and their is a big big tree. it covers half of the neighborhood. Their is a lot of homes and their is a sewer beside us.

Jimmy (whose mother is white, and whose father is black):

In my neighborhood some people are nice and some are mean. There are a lots of trees in my neighborhood. In front of my house people threw trash on the ground and my dad have to pick it up. Across the street there is a park and the park is brooken and we can't play on it. At night time it's quiet because people are asleep. I'm scared of the dark because everytime the light is out my brother scares me. My neighborhood is loud because there are guns, shooting, and there is dogs barking. Black people hangout by the store and my mom is scared because she don't like that store. My dad go there to get milk. People do donuts in cars just to be funny and my family don't like it.

This writing—from *third-graders*—was eye-opening for someone who, every day, was able to go from working in this neighborhood to a quiet, safe home nearby, but essentially in a different world. When I think about what I would have written about my neighborhood at this age, it is very different. I would have probably written about my family and my pets, and maybe about the games I liked to play at recess and the playground I visited with my family on the weekend.

I certainly wouldn't have written about rape, I didn't know anyone who'd been killed, and my neighborhood rarely felt scary.

I asked parents about the park being "broken." It turned out there was a nice park that the city put in for the kids in the projects, but it wasn't safe to play in because people had been assaulted and killed there. It looked nice, though.

Need Versus Want, From Kids Growing Up in East Oakland

I know a park is not technically a need. It's not like food or shelter or clothing. But I tend to think of it as a basic need for children. However, like many people, I sometimes overuse the word "need." I have a tendency to say that I need the new iPhone or I need a pedicure, even though those are clearly just things that I want.

My greatest lesson on distinguishing between wants and needs came with my first grade class during my first year of teaching. Volunteers from the business world came to our school through the Junior Achievement program to teach for a day. As a new teacher, I was overwhelmed and relieved to not be responsible for lesson plans for one day. However, I was nervous about how an idealistic businessperson would deal with twenty extremely needy first graders living in one of the most violent parts of Oakland.

The woman who showed up at my class was clearly unnerved to be in this particular neighborhood. When she walked in, she was shaking slightly and she stammered the first few times the kids asked her a question. But she collected herself quickly enough, and taught in an enthusiastic and respectful manner after that. She went over the official Junior Achievement curriculum, which included basic map skills and identifying the different essential parts of a city.

Then she got to "needs versus wants."

I don't remember exactly how it fit into the lesson as a whole, but I can still picture the images she used: cut-outs of an ice cream cone, roller skates, a house, a plate of food, a t-shirt, etc. The class was supposed to vote on whether each item was a "need" or a "want" and the picture was then taped to that side of the board. For some of the items, there was clear consensus. Everyone agreed that while roller skates and bicycles were nice to have, they were definitely not necessities, so those items went on the "wants" side of the board. Others required some explanation. Ice cream was supposed to be a "want," as it's a treat, but the plate of food represented food as a whole, which went under "needs."

The businesswoman seemed happy with the class discussion and the decisions the kids were making as a group, right up until she got to the picture of the house. The class collectively decided it belonged on the "wants" side. The guest teacher looked confused and then clarified that this image included apartments also, which was quick thinking on her part. But the kids were still not sold. "That's a want," many insisted. The woman looked at her notes and clarified that it was supposed to be a need. "People need homes."

One six-year-old saw her confusion and helpfully jumped in with an explanation. "My uncle don't have a home," she said. "And he still alive." Other kids started jumping in:

"My friend live in a shelter; she don't have a home."
"Some of my family members homeless."
"My mama used to live on the street, but when she had kids she moved to my auntie's house."

One after another, at least half the class shared their anecdotes about homelessness and they all agreed: homes are a "want."

My guest was taken aback—this had not fit into the cookie-cutter script she'd been given. These kids were young enough that most of them were not fully aware how shameful mainstream society considers homelessness to be. They definitely didn't like it, but for them it was a normal part of life.

After school that day, the guest teacher stayed to talk to me and began to cry. She said she had never thought about this kind of poverty existing in the Bay Area. She pointed out that none of the students "looked homeless," as they were all clean and wearing nice clothes.

She was also confused why I hadn't corrected them; she thought they should know that homes were a need.

I didn't agree, though. I thought the kids had a good point.

A Dream to Build Tomorrow On

The rough neighborhood they lived in didn't stop my students from dreaming big, if in an unconventional way for typical third graders. During my fifth year of teaching, for Martin Luther King's birthday, the kids wrote about their dreams. These writing samples went through the entire classroom editing process including peer review, teacher review, and final drafts, so their spelling and grammar has (mostly) been corrected.

TJ:
I have a dream fighting other kids. I have a dream hurting somebody on the football field. I have a dream about running away from home, school, and my football team and when I came back everything was alright.

Jamila:
I have a dream that people will stop smoking and drinking, stop shooting people, stop stealing money, and stop hating people. I wish that Martin Luther King, Jr. was alive. I wish people would stop mugging people.

Marcel:
I have a dream that people would give dogs and cats good homes. I have a dream that people would stop being on drugs. I have a dream that people would respect their homes. I have a dream that people would give people in Africa some food. And I have a dream people would stop killing and fighting.

Kobe:
I have a dream that nobody was on drugs, that nobody killed each other and that no one got raped. I have a dream that my mom does not have diabetes and that I do not hear gun shots and that everything is OK.

The last child in this list, Kobe, moved out of Oakland not long after he wrote this. Two years earlier, his father was shot and killed. During the year that Kobe was in my third grade class, someone came to his apartment to threaten the life of his sixteen-year-old brother. Unwilling to risk losing anyone else in her family the way she'd lost her children's father, the boys' mom decided she'd had enough. So she packed up her kids and moved them over a period of just three days.

We all missed Kobe—he was a wonderful, sweet child—but he may have needed to leave to stay that way. I hope he found somewhere better. His description of himself below (unedited) always made me smile when it was up on the wall in my classroom:

> My name is Kobe. I am 8 years old and my birthday was born in 1998. My eye is dark brown and my hair is black and I like to play footbal. I like to play with my best friend. I am very talkative and honest. I am very cook [cool] and I am very nice. I make friends. I like school. Sometimes I get to change my card to Green that mean I am in trouble. Sometimes I stay on Blue. I got friends and we went to the coliseum the A's won the other day the other day the raider lost. I like school. I have a nice teacher.

Kobe epitomized everything I loved about teaching third grade. He was up-front about his feelings, excited about school and any kind of attention, and just beginning to recognize that actions have consequences.

Romance and Logic in the Third Grade

One of the best things about teaching third grade is that this is the age when most kids are just beginning to develop their critical thinking skills.

I remember one of my students, Denise, posing an excellent question. She asked, "When boys like you, why do they hit you and tease you and call you names and steal your stuff? Why can't they just say they like you?" Then she asked the real kicker: "And when do they stop acting like that?" I had to break it to her that some of them never stop.

I remember Denise as a particularly thoughtful and kind little girl. She showed a deep level of caring about how others were feeling, and always did her best to cheer people up when they were sad. A few weeks after school ended, I got a voicemail from her. She said, "Ms. Harris, I just wanted to call to see how you was doing and if you was having a good summer." That afternoon, I had visited a plaque honoring a college friend of mine who had committed suicide. Denise, of course, had no idea that her cheery voicemail came at exactly the time I needed it, but she had the knack to time it just right somehow.

Another time, she asked me a pointed question that I found particularly astute during a lesson on Christopher Columbus.

"Why do we call them [Native Americans] Indians when India is a different country?" she asked. I told her it was because Columbus was trying to find a new way to get to India, but he got lost and went to America instead. Only he didn't know he was lost. He assumed he had made it to India just fine, so he called the people he met there Indians.

Denise stared at me incredulously. "They got named the wrong thing because he got *lost*?" she asked, then thought for a minute. "And where does he get off naming them anyway? Who said the white guy could name them?"

This kind of critical thinking is not unheard of for a child this young, but it is unusual. To this day, Denise refuses to accept any injustice. She has been involved with the Black Lives Matter movement and uses social media to educate people about the inequity of the much higher rates of incarceration for black men compared to other men in the United States. I could see back when she was in my class how her profound sensitivity and capacity for thoughtful critique of the world around her caused her pain, given the unjust society we live in. But these qualities are also what continue to drive her to work toward positive change today.

The D.C. Diaries

There were many children who were simply a joy to teach. I had a student named Elijah who was incredibly smart and good natured but who liked to complain. He was self-aware enough to realize this and wrote a nice essay at the end of third grade about how he wasn't going to "make a pout" in fourth grade.

Fortunately, his maturity level continued to advance, and in the eighth grade, he even got the chance to meet President Obama. Like many 12-year-old boys would be, Elijah was charmingly unclear as to how this opportunity came about in the first place. When he first told me about his trip, he said, "I got good grades, so I got to meet the president."

He was also uncertain about which actual program it was that had sponsored the trip. What was crystal clear, though, was that Elijah had grown into an amazing kid who was working very hard toward building a brighter future for himself. And he did indeed get to meet the president. Even I was jealous. The following essay, which I'm including unedited here (with the permission of Elijah, now a young adult), is what he wrote in his own words after returning from his trip to Washington, DC.

Before I talk about my trip, I want to ask this question. The question is if you had one shot, or one opportunity, to seize everything you ever wanted, one moment, would you capture it or let it slip? (Eminem, "Lose Yourself") Well, I took my opportunity. It took a lot of hard work, but I got it done. Now it's time to tell you about my trip to D.C.

It all started one day in class. I was in advisory when this man came up to me named Mr. M. He came and took me out of class to talk to me for 5 minutes on if I want to go to Washington D.C. When he told me, I didn't know what to say. I was scared that I would have stage fright, even though I'm not going to be on stage, to meet the president. But instead, I realized that this will help me get into the school I want which is UC Berkeley, and have people proud of me so I said yes.

When my mom came home at 8:35, I told her the good news. She was excited for me and told me that I can go and since I was one of the two from my school going. She said I had to represent my school. A week later, it's time for the big trip. I bring my luggage to Mr. M's office and went to class. Now at 12:50, I leave my 6th period class. My mom comes to tell me, "Don't be over there acting ignorant," kissed me on the cheek and gave me ninety dollars. Soon she left and I left with this one kid from my school and two others. We all got to the plain and took off. The plane sucked, but I was able to get all my work done.

When I got to my room, I had met up with some of my roommates from different schools. They were cool and fun. The weird thing was that they were different. Even though my best friends are just like me, it was cool to hang out with others that were different. When I got to my dorm, it was 3:00 in the morning. I went straight to bed. The next day, in the morning, I always went to this breakfast room that sucked. They had weird things like broccoli and eggs mixed together, something you don't see people eat every day. After I just went around town and checked out D.C.

At night time we played in a place where I played one of my favorite sports which was air hockey. The place was the rec room. The next day I went to some museums and just bought gifts. I saw the Empire State building[10] up close and this Indian culture museum. On Friday, we practiced on how we are going to talk to first the person that works for the Senator of the US and I went on the White House Tour. Oh yeah, we also everyday only ate beef burgers and fries to every meal we ate a restaurant (except breakfast). We ate at a lot of restaurants, one of the names was Hard Rock!

On Saturday, it's now the big day. I look as spiffy as I can. So I'm in, I'm officially talking to Mr. Obama, the President of the United States. When I was talking to him, I asked him

---

[10] He might have meant the Washington Monument.

many questions. One of them was why do private schools get more money than public schools? Are they better than us? He laughed, but he couldn't answer for some reason. What I noticed was he was no different from us today. Except he's not ignorant and mean towards others.

After I was done we had went to this event called National Youth Summit. At that event I saw some actors, some singers, and others. The point of the summit was to involve students to the situation of us not being able to graduate and succeed in life. After it was all said and done, it was time to eat my final beef burger and fries. I knew I wasn't going to have a beef pattie until the upcoming Thanksgiving or New Year's Eve. It was going to be hard but I can get through that. The hard thing was leaving my new friends. Time for me to say the final goodbye to my roommates. I said bye, hugged them (hand shake) and told them I was going to miss them.

So I went back home and they did too. When I got picked up, my mom was excited to see the pictures and know about what happened on the trip. Since I forgot to tell Mr. M thank you for taking me on this trip, I called him. I told him, "I am very thankful for taking me on this trip." He said, "It wasn't me that gave you this opportunity, it was you." I still said thank you, he said you're welcome, and we hung up. This trip started to get to my head that I learned not just how to be confident in words, but also confident in what I can accomplish.

THE END

P.S. Yes I did have jet lag after the trip.

The Darndest Things Indeed

Another thing I love about third graders is the way they use language and where exactly their train of thought goes, sometimes derailing altogether. During a science lesson once, I was teaching the kids about skeletons, and a child raised his hand, looking thoughtful. "Ms. Harris," he said, "if you used one of those hoses that a fireman has, and you put it on a baby, would it lift up the baby into the air? Do babies have bones?"

You just never know what you're going to get from a child's brain, or how it's going to be described.

In one assignment, my students were asked to pick something and describe it, using as many of their senses as possible. The things the kids picked to describe ranged from people (me, their mom, a sibling, etc.), to flowers, dogs and cats, a Game Boy, and crackers. One of my favorite descriptions to ever come from student writing was that crackers "sound like rocks when they break."

One girl wrote (unedited):

> "My sister is Brown like me. She is nice sometimes. She was in my teacher's class last year. She has short and kind of short hair. She smells like soap. She helps grandma clean up the house, because she likes cleaning up the house. I love my sister. My grandma loves my sister. I do too. My sister is the best."

They described things they loved—mostly family members and pets. I couldn't help but be impressed with their outside-the-box descriptions. A few other memorable excerpts (edited) include:

> Robbie: I have a dog that is brown, cool, and hot with fleas. We give him food. We give him flea baths. We keep him away from cats and birds. He smells like junk. He feels like a hairball.

> Brian: My dog can bark very loud because he is twenty-two years old. He smells like mud and is as soft as a pillow.

> Johnny: My dog Fluffy has little legs and sharp teeth. He is the size of a toy. Fluffy is fluffy.

Perhaps for obvious reasons, this one was my favorite:

> Adrian: My teacher smells like perfume. She is light skinned. She is skinny. She is the tallest woman in the school. She sounds loud and quiet. Her hair is light brown. My teacher's hair is so soft. Her eyes are green and beautiful. Her bones in her hand feel bumpy. She wears glasses because she has bad vision. She sprained her ankle because she fell down the stairs and she had to use crutches. My teacher is the best teacher in the world.

I neither wore perfume nor was the tallest woman in the school, but I didn't mind him thinking so.

Things You Hope You Never Hear From a Third Grader

And to leave you with something that always makes me smile, here are a handful of my favorite least favorite things the kids ever said while I was their teacher.

1. "My mama says I need to bring energy drinks to school so I can have more energy!"
2. "I don't need no Kleenex."
3. "I don't have a bedtime 'cause I'm grown."
4. "The pee just came out! I didn't know it was coming."
5. "But he *wanted* me to hit him!"
6. "But it was only a little bit of a stick and I really thought it would go over her head, honest!"
   And finally . . .
7. "Teacher, I don't feel so good . . . Hey, look. I can see what I ate for lunch!"

CHAPTER 10:

JORGE

"One of the most sincere forms of respect
is actually listening to what another has
to say.**"**

—BRYANT H. MCGILL

The Exploratorium

All teachers have children they go the extra mile for, even when they are no longer in their class. It's not possible to do it for all of them, and not all of them need it. My fellow teachers and I are often involved in the lives of special former students outside of school, whether through outings, tutoring, educational or emotional support, or sometimes just cheerleading a kid through his or her struggles and successes.

Jorge was one of those kids for me.

I remember Jorge as an incredibly intelligent child with a beautiful soul, who had the misfortune of being the most responsible "adult" in his family by age seven. His father was absent and his mother spent a lot of time in rehab, jail, or living with her boyfriend outside the family home.

Jorge's grandmother was the guardian for him and his four younger siblings, but she was remarkably hands off when it came to child-rearing. She also didn't speak any English, and was illiterate in Spanish. So it was up to Jorge to sign all forms (his grandmother couldn't write her own name), deal with people over the telephone, get his brother and himself to and through school, and oftentimes feed himself and his siblings. Under the weight of these responsibilities, he carried tension that no child should have to bear; you could see it in his face and in the droop of his head and shoulders.

He also worried a lot about his mother, who'd had him as a teenager. He adored her and also felt responsible for her. One day in third grade, he told me he had stayed up all night because she'd gotten in the car drunk and hadn't come home, and he didn't know if she was hurt, in jail, sleeping somewhere else, or dead. He tried all night to figure out if he should call the police or if that would only get her in more trouble.

In my second to last year of teaching, Mr. Jackson (a friend who had volunteered in my class) and I took Jorge and his younger brother, Luis, to the Exploratorium, a hands-on science museum in San Francisco. Jorge had been in my third-grade class the year before, and Luis was in first grade. Two adults to two children was the perfect ratio for a fun, flexible trip, especially because the two boys moved at such different paces. Luis wanted to run from exhibit to exhibit (which he called "games"), while Jorge wanted to spend time at each one, asking questions and determined to understand how each of them worked.

While we explored interactive exhibits that involved light, sound, engines, cows' eyes, weather, water, colors, and optical illusions—basically everything a kid could ever want to learn about—I mostly stayed with Luis, while my friend patiently answered Jorge's questions. We stayed at the museum until we were all completely saturated, and then we went to Ocean Beach in San Francisco.

These kids had only been to the beach once before, with another teacher. I asked if they wanted to build sand castles, and Jorge admitted he didn't know how. That simply wouldn't do, Mr. Jackson and I decided, so we went on a frenzy of beach activity—building sand castles, digging moats, writing the kids' names in the sand, and racing along the water's edge, lingering past our intended departure time.

I still have photos from that day, and they are bittersweet. I love seeing how carefree the boys were, even as I'm heartbroken knowing that childhood freedom was a rarity for them. That day, at least, was full of sand and smiles out under the sun.

Teenage Struggles

When Jorge was thirteen, he started to crack under the pressure of his life circumstances. That age is never really fun, no matter who you are. But the challenges he faced made it harder. On the positive side, his family life was improving. He didn't have to look after Luis as much. And his mom and dad were each (separately) becoming more involved in his life, though both still had a tendency to flake out when he needed them.

Around this time, Jorge began dating a girl several years older than him—a high-school dropout already aged beyond her sixteen years. He often fought with his mother and grandmother, sometimes saying awful things to them. His temper was volatile, and he could lose control easily when angry, knocking over chairs and tables and breaking things.

Compounding the challenges at home, he got into trouble at school. Jorge was attending a large, older middle school with a reputation as a dumping ground for students whose parents didn't know (or care) that there were alternatives. There, he started dressing and acting like a stereotypical wannabe gangster: wearing sagging pants and a hoodie or beanie to hide his face, cursing at strangers, and not acting much more civil to the people he did know.

His teachers looked for any possible excuse to kick Jorge out of class. And he gave them plenty, from flicking rubber bands, to wrestling in the hall, to talking back and even once claiming he had a gun (he didn't). The school tried to expel him, but Mr. Jackson and I brought Jorge and his mother to the hearing and the teacher and principal didn't show up, so Jorge "won."

We also went to a meeting with Jorge's counselor and acting principal—they were between principals—and explained his home situation, how he was desperately behind and wasn't getting the help he needed, and how that contributed to his acting out. (It's far less humiliating to get kicked out of class for threatening a teacher than to have everyone see you can't read very well.) Both the acting principal and the counselor promised to do everything in their power to assist him with counseling, extra math and reading help, checking on him personally, and helping him get organized. They gave us their email addresses and phone numbers and urged us to follow up. We left in high spirits.

But our optimism was short lived, as it became clear that the school officials would never answer any of my (many) follow-up inquiries. They didn't take the time and energy to really see or respond to the situation. Jorge, like most children (and adults), was very sensitive to respect or the lack thereof, and he knew that his teachers didn't respect him. Nor did they have time for him.

By his reasoning, that meant they didn't deserve his respect either.

I was frustrated that the counselor and the school made promises to help him that they couldn't or just didn't keep. At the same time, I understand what they were up against. They had a school full of students who were almost statistically certain not to succeed and, under the No Child Left Behind Act, they were facing funding cuts along with more mandates. I know from experience how exhausting it is to really give these kids what they need, because they need *a lot*. But if the adults who have taken on the responsibility of educating these kids can't keep their basic promises of support, they should step aside for people who will.

Jorge did end up switching schools, and much to my surprise and delight, the change was like night and day. I got a phone call from his new assistant principal, saying that Jorge had named me among the supportive adults he had in his life who were looking out for him. Over the next week, I got positive emails from Jorge's principal, assistant principal, counselor, and a couple of teachers.

The minute they met him, they somehow saw his potential, and he responded. (Really, I *promise:* kids will live up—or down—to your expectations.) In email after email, I read that he was respectful, on time, working hard, and accepting help in getting more organized. Each correspondent seemed to honestly care about this kid who had been in their school for only a week.

I decided to meet the assistant principal and check up on Jorge. Now, I had seen a lot of middle schools in this district, but this one felt like entering the Twilight Zone.

It was clean. It was bright. Instead of graffiti everywhere, the grounds boasted a beautiful mural made by students. Jorge was called out of his class to talk to us and . . . I honestly don't know how to describe it. I wish I had a before and after picture. He was wearing a uniform: khaki pants and a white shirt. He wasn't sagging his pants. There was nothing hiding his face. He wasn't slouching. And he was *smiling.* He looked like a different kid. He was standing up straight for the first time in years.

Jorge told me that he was getting help on his multiplication tables—and for once, he wasn't angry and didn't call himself stupid for not knowing them. When the assistant principal broached the subject of maybe repeating eighth grade because he had all F's up until the school change, Jorge explained to us why it would be a good idea for him. He told me about a field trip that he was taking to various University of California campuses. The change was astounding.

This was not a kid who trusted easily. That whole first week, if he'd had an inkling that a teacher didn't want him there or didn't respect him, he would have been right back to his old habits. I was blown away by how incredible the staff must be for him to respond so well.

I was so thankful that he found his way there. However, help with multiplication and organization—or even repeating eighth grade—weren't going to be enough to prepare him for the challenges still to come.

Tragedy by Numbers

Shortly after Jorge switched schools, Mr. Jackson and I treated him, Luis, and their friend Johnny to dinner. I remembered Johnny—an eighth grader at this time—from when he went to East Oakland Elementary, although he was never in my class. He was a bit of a troublemaker and was on probation from an arrest earlier that year. But unlike most kids I've known who have been in this kind of trouble, he was up front about everything.

Johnny spoke of his regret over what he'd done and said he was learning not to hang around people who did "stupid stuff." He also told us what crack had done to some of his friends, how gross it was, and how he'd rather not be around it. By this time, I had learned to tell when kids were lying, and he wasn't. He wanted to turn his life around. He gave me a hug for taking him out to eat.

That was the last time I would see Johnny.

A week after our outing, Johnny was killed by another teenager. Jorge had been lucky to escape the shooting. Jorge and his girlfriend were walking with Johnny right by Jorge's grandmother's house when two brothers shot at them.

Jorge and Luis said the younger brother (age thirteen) shot at them and missed, and then the older brother (seventeen) shot Johnny. Jorge's girlfriend took off running, and Jorge tried to help his friend while running away himself. Johnny collapsed across the street from Jorge and Luis's grandmother's house. Luis ran out of the house to see what was happening and the two brothers, together, watched one of their best friends die.

As if that weren't enough trauma for the night, the police investigation only made things harder on Jorge and Luis.

After the shooting, the police took Jorge and Luis,

Community altar to honor Johnny the day after his murder.

with no attempt to conceal their identities, to point out the house where the suspects lived. As a result, the suspects' entire family saw exactly who "ratted them out." Then the officers took Jorge and Luis to the police station and kept them there for nearly six hours, until four in the morning. Though the boys' parents were called, Jorge and Luis weren't allowed to talk to them or have them in the room during questioning—at least not until a lawyer got involved.

Tragically, it turns out that Jorge and Luis's mom had complained to the police six months earlier about one of the suspects in Johnny's murder after he threatened her son with a gun. The police came to the house and reportedly told her, "If no one is dead, we can't do anything."

Now someone was dead.

Really? We had to wait for that to happen before anything could be done? What happened to Johnny (and by extension, to Jorge, Luis, their families, and their community) is a tragic example of why it is so important for police officers to know the people and communities they serve. It's possible that these police officers had seen all too many stories like this one playing out before, and believed nothing could be done, or that they simply had no more emotion or energy left to give. In any case, what happened was devastating, and to this day I can't shake the thought that it didn't have to happen this way.

The next morning, Mr. Jackson and I went to see how the kids were doing. Not surprisingly, they were devastated. But things went from bad to worse when a police officer came by that morning with a search warrant, searched for a gun (but didn't find one), and took Jorge away with him without letting his mother come along. His mother tried to ask why they were taking her son, but she only spoke Spanish and could not understand the officers.

Thankfully, a lawyer friend who also knew the kids came and saved the day, at least temporarily, by making sure that Jorge had representation and was not questioned again without his mother present.

I was horrified and sickened by the online comments responding to the news article about Johnny's death. Many simply wrote him off, saying "Well, he lived in the ghetto, and that's what happens." I realize that gang and drug violence are responsible for a lot of deaths. But this kid was just walking home. Is it just too hard to negotiate a frightening world unless you can convince yourself that only "bad" children or children from "bad places" become victims?

It sounds morbid, but as a teacher in East Oakland, I always wondered which of the school's children would be the first to get killed. You know it's always a possibility in that area. But I thought he'd be older than thirteen.

I grieved for Johnny, and I grieved for Jorge and Luis who had seen him killed and may never feel whole again after such a traumatic experience.

The After-Effects of Trauma

As Jorge, Luis, and their family began processing the grief and trauma of witnessing the murder of a friend, the boys would often exhibit overblown emotional outbursts over seemingly little things.

I worried about them. Jorge talked about getting an AK-47 and shooting anyone who bothered him. He had long been in the habit of saying such things for dramatic effect, but now the comments were both more frequent and more violent. Luis picked up on his brother's habit, too. When he borrowed my sleeping bag for summer camp, he plotted his response if other campers wouldn't help him pack up the bag, saying, "If they don't help me, I'll just shoot them."

This may be "normal" for kids who had recently witnessed the killing of a close friend, but it was really hard to hear. I don't think they had any access to guns, fortunately, but violence was definitely on their minds. Both boys were dead set against much-needed counseling. Jorge waved it off with a macho, "I ain't retarded."

Their mother, Sara, remained extremely strong for her kids. She had faced many difficulties, and hadn't always been able to be there for them, so—understandably—they rebelled against her. Still, she did a pretty good job providing consistency and enforcing rules, hard to do when your teenaged son who's bigger than you is screaming in your face.

Jorge's anger continued to escalate over the months following the murder. As a young child, this boy was thoughtful, caring, and more responsible than any kid his age should ever have to be. But after Johnny's murder, he talked about wanting to kill the person who had killed his friend. "I'm gonna go and get me a gun," he'd say. "I'm gonna leave and not come back."

I was never too worried about the running away part because, as Mr. Jackson pointed out, if he were really going to run away, he'd simply do it instead of threatening it via text message three times in one day. What was more troubling was his growing apathy and lack of desire to do the things that had previously brought him joy.

Free summer camp? No. Camping? No. Working for money? No. Going to Waterworld? No. At that point, you could have offered him a trip to anywhere in the world, with a million dollars thrown in, and I think he'd have turned it down.

Jorge used to talk a lot—not a chatterbox conversationalist, but delighting in shocking people by listing all the inappropriate things he was going to do. In response, I would hand him food and make a joke about putting food in his mouth to have some quiet and he'd think it was funny. After Johnny's death, Jorge's response to most things was violence, anger, and sullen silence. When he was called out on this new attitude, his response was simply, "Oh, well."

As my relationship and conversations with him began to erode, Jorge texted me repeatedly, asking me to get out of his life and never come back. Were it not for the many years developing a strong foundation of a caring relationship, I probably would have given up and assumed there was no hope for him, the way he was headed. I think he needed frequent reassurance that someone actually cared about him, so he would test me, fervently hoping I wouldn't desert him.

As Jorge was processing it, I, too, was still waiting for it to hit me that one of the kids from East Oakland Elementary School had died violently— the very thing I'd been dreading and praying would never happen, even though it was statistically likely. I didn't know Johnny terribly well, but we were all together the week before he died. I knew he was prone to messing around and getting in trouble and he didn't do well in school, but he was smart, funny, extremely thoughtful, and loved his family fiercely.

Another kid killed him—and nobody else knows why.

Another Bad Decision

A little over a year after Johnny's death, Jorge was arrested for drinking and driving—just weeks after his fourteenth birthday.

He took the car keys while his mother was sleeping and went out with his cousin after the two of them had been drinking. Both were underage, and Jorge obviously had no license. At fourteen, he wasn't even eligible for a learner's permit.

His mom, understandably, freaked out. She already faced incredible challenges to keep her family together. They needed to find a place to move in another month, and they didn't have the money to do it. She was a recovering addict trying to stay clean in the middle of an already difficult situation, just trying to hold things together for her kids.

That car had been a real chance for the family, and it was impounded after the arrest. Sara had bought it so that she could work and not be dependent on government assistance. Jorge's momentary lapse of judgment would have far-reaching consequences for his family, already struggling to keep their heads above water emotionally and financially.

What would Sara and her kids do next month with no job, no money, no place to live, and no car to help her find and keep a job? Just as worrisome was the fact that Jorge had a record—a serious one.

Where would he go from there?

A Beautiful Christmas in the Ghetto

The year Johnny died, my winter break provided a much-needed rest—pleasant but uneventful except for thirty minutes that proved nothing short of a Christmas miracle.

Jorge and Luis had been more or less missing in action leading up to the holidays. Mr. Jackson and I had offered take them out to eat several times, only to have them not home when we showed up at the pre-arranged times. Jorge had changed his cell phone number and not given us the new one, and Luis answered only intermittently.

Mostly cut off, I didn't know what was going on in their lives. So when we finally did confirm a time and place to meet the boys, Mr. Jackson and I were hopeful—if a little skeptical—that we'd actually get to see and spend time with them.

We pondered what to get Jorge and Luis for Christmas on a limited budget. They were eleven and fourteen then, awkwardly between the ages for kids' toys and more grown-up presents. I wasn't sure that anything we chose for them would be well-received.

In the end, we decided on McDonald's and In-N-Out gift certificates, perhaps not the healthiest option, but one that would make them happy. And I'd take happiness anywhere we could find it with these kids.

At the last minute, Mr. Jackson added two remote-controlled cars. I was skeptical—I thought the boys would be in their "we're too grown and too cool for that baby stuff" mode. I was even more nervous because Luis kept texting us asking where his presents were, so I thought his expectations would be overblown and he'd end up disappointed.

We picked up Luis and drove a few blocks to his aunt's house where Jorge was waiting for us. They had grown in our time apart; Jorge was almost as tall as I was at that point (5'8"), and Luis was growing taller and slimming down.

Jorge came out of his aunt's house and said everyone was asleep. We decided to open the presents right there in front of the apartment building—in the ghetto in the dark. The kids got the remote control cars and did what any brothers would do—immediately started driving the cars into each other.

Those cars fell off the curb, went into the road, and repeatedly crashed into each other. Eventually Jorge realized he was trying to control the wrong car, which led to all manner of hilarity. Then we gave them their Christmas cards with the gift certificates. The kids read every word of the Christmas cards—I could see them moving their lips—and asked if they really could get food from McDonald's and In-N-Out. Luis reacted as though our choice had been inspired by mind reading or divine intervention, not the constant stream of his asking for McDonald's every time we saw him for the past four years.

Then we gave the kids gingerbread houses. A friend had bought icing and candy, baked up a bunch of gingerbread, and invited people over for a decorating party. I decided to bring the decorated houses to the boys along with some extra frosting and candy so they could add their own layer of sugary goodness.

We left and they took all the loot inside, and a few minutes later, Jorge texted us asking if we could make a gingerbread mansion. A gingerbread mansion!

That was not the request of a tough, mean teenager from the ghetto waiting to go to juvenile hall. That was the kid I had known for seven years. That was a kid getting to be a kid again, if only for a little while.

Later that night, he texted me "Thank you for the gifts." After a year of being cursed out and told to go away, that thank you meant more to me than any other I had ever received.

Then he told me he was eating the gingerbread houses and asked again if we could please make a gingerbread mansion. That made me sublimely happy—that and holding on to the beautiful image of him crashing his toy car into his brother's and looking honestly content, happy, and at peace, even just for a minute.

It was a brief, blessed escape from his everyday worries: whether his mom would make enough money for food, or if she would get drunk again, or if he was going to go to juvenile hall, or if his girlfriend was pregnant.

No fourteen-year-old should have such worries. But in his neighborhood, those realities and fears were and still are commonplace for teens.

But having gotten to see that loving, silly, thankful side of him again—even for just thirty minutes—I felt as though that would offset another six months of his heartbreaking anger and despair, because I knew that he also had good memories and would know that there were people around him who loved him.

A New Heartbreak

After years of being completely out of touch with the boys, I searched for them through Google and social media. There was one hit, and the article I found was devastating: Jorge had been arrested for the attempted murder of an Oakland police officer. With the assistance of a friendly reporter, I learned that no one had actually been physically harmed in this altercation, but that Jorge received a nineteen-year sentence in San Quentin.

When I learned Jorge's fate, the hopeless, helpless despair I felt was devastating. Jorge had been faced with issues too large, difficult, and painful for him to bear from the moment he was born. He was loving, giving and intelligent, but his home, neighborhood, and school beat him down from the beginning.

While I in no way condone his actions, I think I understand them. Jorge had been battling anger at injustice all his life, and something broke when he saw Johnny killed. Like the tragic hero of a Greek play, Jorge was a fundamentally good person in an impossible situation, who made a poor choice and is now paying the price for his actions.

Did he commit a heinous crime? Yes. Did he deserve punishment for it? Yes. Did he receive a stiffer sentence because of his race, economic background, and the quality of the legal representation he received? Almost certainly. But more importantly, how many factors beyond his control contributed to the conditions that led to the crime? What minimal difference in any one of them might have kept him out of this situation to begin with?

What if the police had acted upon Sara's complaint? What if Jorge had lived in a safer community, one with more limited access to guns? What if Jorge's father or another male role model had been in the picture providing guidance on a regular basis? What if school resources had permitted him to get counseling?

Jorge's case is not unique. The environment of violence and deprivation, the lack of concern and resources, the preconception of criminality and unwillingness to truly seek rehabilitation and redemption—these societal choices are working behind the scenes, leading to the inevitability of more Johnnys, more Jorges, more prison sentences, and more San Quentins.

CHAPTER 11:

FRED

"*It's so much darker when a light goes out than it would have been if it had never shone.*"

—JOHN STEINBECK,
The Winter of Our Discontent

A Challenging Student

Another student who wormed his way into my heart more than most was Fred. Fred was "complicated and wonderful," a fitting tribute from one of my classroom volunteers. He was in the first-grade class I taught at East Oakland Elementary during my first year of teaching. And he taught me, in a visceral way, the pain and tragedy of a talented, wounded African-American boy colliding with a system that has limited tolerance for disobedience and too few avenues of help and support.

Our relationship got off to a rocky start. Fred's class had had six substitutes before I arrived in January 2000. Within the first ten minutes of my first day of class, he threw a book at my head, and I had to send him home. That volatility was never far from the surface. He was so angry that it all but oozed out of his pores, even when he was only six years old.

Sometimes his classmates were the target, and Fred would knock over a desk and scream at the rest of the class. Or he would "flinch" (what he called pretending to hit someone) at them to scare them. Other times he would really hit them. This unpredictable and aggressive behavior was effective, and Fred (who was very small for his age) terrorized kids who were older and bigger than he was.

At other times, the anger was self-directed. He'd get terribly mad at himself when he couldn't read something correctly. He'd breathe really hard and turn red in the face. Even when he wanted to calm down, he couldn't—his anger consumed him.

I realized that emotional control was a key underlying issue for Fred and tried to help him recognize what he was feeling and that he had the power to choose how he would react.

But sometimes this child, who was known around school as a terror, would curl into a ball and sob uncontrollably because he didn't know how to deal with all of his feelings. I taught him the word "frustrated," and when he'd get mad, sometimes he'd still act out and scream, "*I . . . am . . . so . . . frustrated!*"

The rest of that year was up and down for us, but we built a solid relationship. I would offer to come see his baseball game (it was T-ball, but he wanted me to call it baseball) and his whole face would light up.

The meltdowns didn't stop, however, and came complete with crying, kicking, screaming, and swearing. I gave him time-outs at the class across the hall, where the teacher would run him through multiplication tables to calm him down. I can still see how proud he was that he had learned 12 x 12 in the first grade. He would alternate stealing my supplies or throwing up gang signs (using gestures related to gangs) in class photos with showing off how well he could read. Progress was two steps forward and one step back, but I think he understood that I cared about him.

Fred's home life was clearly not the source of stability he so desperately needed. His father was in prison (for trying to kill someone, according to Fred) and Fred was angry enough to promise to kill his father if he ever got out. His mother was being abused by her boyfriend, the father of Fred's half-brother and half-sister, and she often showed up at school with bruises on her face. I heard that, during a parent-teacher conference for the younger brother, she tried to speak up and her boyfriend just raised the back of his hand at her like he was going to backhand her across the face. After that, my concerned colleague said Fred's mother stayed quiet through the rest of the meeting.

Although a victim, Fred's mom was also an aggressor. She was fiercely protective and vacillated between "my child can do no wrong" and "Help me. I don't know what to do with him." One day she would tell me that having me as a teacher was the best thing that had ever happened to Fred and she thanked God for me. Another day she would curse at me and accuse me of being out to get her son because I hated black people. I'm sure she had a lot to deal with and I know she loved her son immensely, but her words and actions did not always help him.

So, perhaps by default, I became a safe place for Fred. All through elementary school, he would come in my classroom and say, in a desperate tone, "Ms. Harris, you've got to calm me down! You're the only one who can calm me down."

Sometimes I could, and other times I couldn't. Once, when he was in fifth grade, he was so upset that as he was flailing his body around, he knocked me off balance. He froze and started crying uncontrollably. I had to assure him I was okay and he kept repeating that he never wanted to hurt me. I had never seen him have that reaction before, and I believe it was fear that he might lose one of the few people he could trust.

A Child's Sense of Worth

Fred left East Oakland Elementary in second grade, reputedly for hitting a teacher. I believe he was expelled, but it may have just been a "push-out," where the administration "encouraged" his mom to send him to another school. In third grade he came back to our school, and I, now a third-grade teacher, agreed to take him in, because I thought I was his best chance for success—since I actually wanted him there.

There were some bright spots that year. We connected him with a counseling intern working at the school then, whom he liked. Plus, I had some amazing volunteers that year: athletes from UC Berkeley. One of them, a tennis player named Paul, really took Fred under his wing. Fred looked forward to Fridays when he could see Paul.

Even on the other days, when Paul wasn't physically present, he helped Fred keep a tighter rein on his own turbulent emotions. The counseling intern taught Fred a visualization exercise: to think of something fun and relaxing. So when Fred needed to calm himself down, he would sit in the corner, close his eyes, then deal invisible UNO cards ("one to me, one to Paul"). Wherever Paul is now, I hope he knows how much he impacted Fred.

One day, when Fred was in my third-grade class, he threw a tantrum that was more self-directed than usual. He flailed on the floor and yelled "I hate myself. I'm no good!" crumpled paper, and knocked things over. It was after school, so I let him bluster for a while. Finally, I said, "Fred, we're going to make a list of things that are good about you." He froze. I got on the computer and started typing.

I had no help from Fred at all. He alternately screamed and flailed on the floor (and this wasn't just a temper tantrum; it was obvious that he was in serious emotional pain). But soon he was curious enough to come look at what I was writing. Although I no longer have a copy of the list, I suspect I included things such as "He is a great reader" and "He always respects me." I finished typing and told Fred that I was printing two copies, one for me and one for him, so that we could each remember some good things about him. I told him that these weren't all the good things about him, because that would take way too long. These were just the first ten of many.

I printed Fred's copy and he said, "I don't want your stupid list. There ain't no good things about me!" He crumpled it up and threw it in the empty garbage can. I told him that was fine; he could do whatever he wanted with it. I said that I was keeping mine to remind me of some of the great things about him. He kept repeating that he didn't want "no stupid list." I think he really wanted me to react angrily to justify his own anger, but I stayed calm. He stormed out.

I resumed my work on the computer and heard the door open and someone rustling in the garbage can. When I turned back around, Fred's backpack disappeared though the door. The garbage can was empty again.

The School-to-Prison Pipeline Personified

I lost track of Fred for seven or eight years. I'd heard from another student that he got kicked out of high school for "being bad," but that was all I knew. Then, out of the blue, my friend and former co-worker sent me an email:

> "Hey, I am watching this special on PBS hosted by Tavis Smiley. He is at juvenile hall and I think I just saw Fred. I don't remember his last name but I knew him as soon as I saw him. He had the scar on his forehead. Isn't that your old student? They said he was eighteen. Does that add up?"

Yes, it did add up. Fred (his real name is used in the show, but not here) was featured in Tavis Smiley's *Too Important to Fail* documentary. He looked almost exactly the same, but was surprisingly calmer than I had ever seen him. I emailed the producers of the documentary and got the phone number of the librarian at the juvenile detention facility, who could pass on a message to Fred. It worked. I got a voicemail from Fred saying he was glad to hear from me, he hoped I was doing well, and to call him back. I had no number to call him back so I tried the librarian again a few times but never heard from Fred again.

A year or so later, I saw him very briefly on the streets of Oakland. He looked at me intently and asked if I still had the same phone number as before. I told him I did and he said, "I'ma call you," and drove off.

He never did. I'm not sure if he intended to keep the promise, but I know he never will.

Rosa, one of Fred's classmates at East Oakland Elementary, was volunteering at the organization I worked for, about to return for her senior year at UCLA, when she came into my office one day in 2015 looking downcast. "Ms. Harris," she said, "Do you know Fred's last name?"

I knew immediately what Rosa was going to say. There weren't a lot of reasons that she would have brought up Fred. And honestly, this was a likely outcome for him. But more than that, I just knew. I felt a sinking in the pit of my stomach as she told me that Fred had been shot and killed that week in East Oakland. I wasn't surprised, but I was still heartbroken.

Rosa showed me a brief news article about a young man who'd been killed, confirming what I already knew in my gut: the young man was Fred. I'm grateful to her for the kindness of telling me herself, sparing me the shock of finding out about his death on the news. She knows how much I love "my kids," even once they're grown.

When I learned what had happened to Fred, I told my co-workers that I needed some time to myself and, as anyone raised in Oakland would have, they understood. They had all lost classmates, friends, or family to this kind of violence.

I have since heard from a reputable source that at that time, Fred was trying to get out of the gang life, and that he had started going to job training not long before he was gunned down. I don't know if this was true, or even if it matters. No one deserves to die violently. I knew and loved this child, who barely got to become a young man. I saw the potential he had and how much he wanted to be something other than what he was.

It breaks my heart that he couldn't get out of this life before the violence caught up with him.

A Culture of Intervention and Redemption

The Tavis Smiley documentary that featured Fred's story shows how difficult it is for black boys and young men in this country. It would have made me cry even if I didn't know any of the young men involved in the project, because this is such a hard truth.

Any of the other young men in the documentary might as well have been my students. They had experienced loss and anger and made bad decisions, but probably hadn't had the tools to deal with the emotions and situations that resulted. They were disappointed in themselves, and they could clearly state how they had ended up incarcerated. Many of them had lived their lives surrounded by violence and didn't know any alternative. Many were told from an early age that they were "bad." They internalized the message that society had no use for them, making the odds slim to none for any of them having a job or other role where they could be rewarded for contributing to society.

Fred was the second to last young man to speak in the clip from the documentary that I first saw. In it, he speaks thoughtfully and intelligently about wanting better for himself than the things he'd done and where he was at that point in his life. I don't know what he was locked up for, how many times it happened, or what changed or didn't change in his mind and heart, but I had prayed for him for ten years before seeing this documentary.

Fred's story both breaks my heart and reminds me of why I am so grateful and honored to have had the chance to teach where I did. As an adult, I'm sure Fred realized that the world, in many ways, is even more unfair than he imagined it to be as a child. But I hope he also knew, somehow, that there were still people who believed in him and believed that he was more than the sum total of his anger.

Too Important to Fail gives anyone who's tempted to judge imprisoned kids the opportunity to actually listen to them. Of course these young adults have made mistakes and bad decisions—in some cases, decisions that caused a great deal of pain. But there's always a reason and a story behind the action that landed them in juvenile hall. These stories don't absolve them of responsibility for their actions, but they do show there is plenty of blame to go around and that it is up to us to stop this cycle.

Part of that means reforming a judicial system in which low-income young men of color often receive more frequent and harsher prison sentences for the same types of crimes compared to more affluent and/or white offenders. Harsher mandatory sentencing laws adopted during

America's "War on Drugs" are partially to blame for this. Additionally, public defenders are often under-resourced and thus, as a consequence, unprepared, even when they are dedicated and competent. This too needs to change.

Kids who grow up in places like East Oakland are too often viewed as a burden on society because of the costs related to incarceration and violence. But if we could get to them sooner, with real alternatives, and prove their value to themselves and the greater world around them, perhaps they could stand a chance. Even Fred, who had incredible disadvantages in where he was born and in his early family and school life, who made bad decisions and paid for them, was able to redeem himself and start on a different path. And yet he still wound up dead, as do so many of his black and brown brothers who never make it out of the vortex of violence swirling around our prisons and inner-city neighborhoods.

This tragic reality and the lives it continues to destroy break my heart, and yet the challenge remains clear. We must remake our society to help kids like Fred navigate the hurdles of an unjust society.

CHAPTER 12

BURNING OUT AND A BETTER MODEL

"*If you're not really committed, maybe you should get out of education.***"**

—MY PRINCIPAL,
   when I went home with strep throat.

Reaching the Breaking Point

When I was teaching in East Oakland, many people didn't understand why I was always so tired after work. "But you get off at three in the afternoon, and you only work for nine months of the year," they'd say. Before long, I got so tired of hearing people say this that I began snapping at even the most well-intentioned among them.

School may have been out for the day at three, but that didn't mean my work day was over. On any given day, there were still after-school meetings, grading, tutoring, home visits, lesson preparation, purchasing and creating materials . . . and the list goes on. For many teachers, all this extra work before and after hours (at school or at home) comes in addition to the work of caring for their families. On our salaries, many teachers can't afford after-school care for their own kids.

Being exhausted at the end of the day was par for the course. First, I was constantly on the go. Most days, I couldn't even get two minutes free to go to the bathroom until the kids left. Indeed, bladder infections are a common occupational hazard among teachers for this reason.

With only a thirty-minute lunch period, I usually didn't eat lunch until after school either. My colleagues and I routinely found that once you figure in time spent walking kids to lunch, getting the room ready for the next activity, making copies, and getting homework ready, there is usually no time left to eat.

In addition to being physically exhausted, my mental energy was also stretched thin—mostly by the adults at the school, not the kids. The demands placed upon the school's teachers by the administration had become overwhelming.

I was tired of sending kids to the office after I had exhausted every possible disciplinary action in the classroom, only to have them sent back because none of the administrators were equipped to deal with them; tired of meetings that gobbled up teachers' precious time without getting anything useful done; tired of spending *thousands* of dollars of my own money (literally; I kept track) each year on supplies and trips that the school or district should have been paying for; tired of the crazy amounts of paperwork we had to do, and of the ludicrous standardized testing schedule that negatively impacted students and teachers alike; tired of feeling I had to tackle everything on my own, without the support of my administrators or even a senior colleague to provide mentorship.

Secondhand Trauma

On top of being physically and mentally exhausted, I was also emotionally exhausted.

To be an effective teacher, you always have to be enthusiastic, understanding, firm, and at least somewhat entertaining—all at the same time. Being "on" all the time gets physically and emotionally tiring. But working under the conditions we faced as teachers at East Oakland Elementary compounded this strain exponentially.

First, there was the extra weight of witnessing and dealing with the incredibly difficult circumstances so many of my students were grappling with. Like secondhand smoke, that secondhand trauma impacted me as well.

Day in and day out, students came to school reeling from the latest hardships their families were facing. Gang violence, incarceration, drug use, hunger, poverty, abuse, and evictions were all a normal part of life for the adults in their lives—which meant they were far too common in these kids' lives too. Most of the adults I know would have a terribly difficult time coping with these issues, let alone being faced with such challenges as kids. Yet the school administration made no allowances for entire communities of kids who routinely faced such hardships.

The worst of what the kids went through haunted me both in and out of the classroom. Some of it *still* haunts me to this day, a decade later— like the day one of my students told me his dad had threatened to hurt him in ways that made even the Social Services worker I talked to about it cry. And like most kids in his situation, when Social Services showed up at his house, he got in big trouble.

The next day he said to me, "I want to tell you about what goes on in my house, but you have to promise not to tell anyone." I told him that everything he tells me is private *except* if anyone's hurting him or if he wants to hurt himself, because the law is that I had to tell someone then, and because I wanted to keep him safe. Even as I said this to him, my heart sank, knowing how little any of us were really able to protect kids like him, because their live-in abusers find out when they have spoken up.

He looked at me and said, "Then you can't help me at all. And no one can help me." Then he put his head down on his desk for the rest of the morning. Later, I found a crumpled piece of paper that had been the beginning of a letter to me—until we had this conversation. It started with, "My parents hurt me and they always do it . . ."

I read this and I wanted to put my head down, too.

I believe that over time, witnessing that much suffering in the children I taught and cared about so much and not being able to provide them with real help was the crux of what wore me down. Soon I was exhausted *all the time.*

The Effects of Inequality and Lack of Leadership

Another thing that wore me down emotionally was the inequality my students faced. No one ever admitted out loud that my students from a poor neighborhood were considered less valuable than their wealthier peers, but the difference in school resources exposed the truth.

The kids in my class were more perceptive than many people gave them credit for—enough so that when inequities arose, the students noticed. When we mapped out which libraries in Oakland were slated for closure, one child asked why all the libraries being closed were all "over by us" and not in the hills. They noticed when the Oakland police took almost an hour to respond to an attempted kidnapping at the school. "If we was white kids up in the hills they would have been there right away," one student said. They saw their broken-down school and their playground that resembled a prison yard more than a play space, and they understood that they simply weren't worth much to the people in charge of the budget.

There was very little support for teachers at East Oakland Elementary, another factor in my burnout. As a result, teacher turnover was incredibly high. Most years, around half of our teachers left. Schools with a strong and supportive leader may be able to recruit strong replacements and make gains, but with eight principals in the eight years I was there, we rarely had a leader with the commitment and engagement to bring in the best teachers.

At one point, the faculty council started meeting to discuss issues with the administration, and we would sometimes spend time at lunch or after school to talk about what needed to change.

For my part, my participation was idealistic; I wanted to bring change and hope to the school. However, the conversations quickly fizzled out as people realized how much work that would take and how drastically the system needed to be overhauled. In addition, the change in leadership every year (sometimes in the middle of the year) posed another complication. By the time we had established any sort of consistency or implemented a plan, a new principal would come along and we'd be back to square one.

With a strong, supportive principal and administration, my story as a public school teacher may have ended very differently. As it was, the never-ending game of musical chairs among the faculty and staff only compounded the other problems with the administration, as well as the challenges inherent in teaching a community of kids whose needs continued to go unaddressed by the system.

Putting My Own Oxygen Mask on First

By the 2006–2007 school year, my exhaustion level was all I could think about during and after work. Barely able to get through the school day, I had no energy left for social interaction and became more and more isolated. Friends became concerned about me and frequently commented that I needed some sort of break, or even a career change. I scheduled my days around being able to take a nap after work every day, because my exhaustion had reached that level. I was constantly sick, and my life revolved only around school and my students.

By that year, even class projects I loved, like our book clubs, had lost their luster. In spite of my pride for my students' increased reading activities and their growing ability to analyze stories and take on leadership positions within their groups, I couldn't facilitate book clubs any more. Those kinds of extras took more energy than I had to give, and my teaching suffered greatly.

During school breaks when I had time off, it was hard to recover. Even with two weeks off for Christmas vacation during my last school year, it wasn't until the last Sunday of the time off that I finally began to feel rested. And then I had to go back to school the next day.

At that point, I finally decided to take my friends' concerns and warnings to heart and try to take care of myself by applying for a leave of absence. This plan would give me a chance to see if I could recover my health. And it would leave me the option of being able to go back after a year—if I could.

So in January 2007, I applied for a leave of absence for the 2007–2008 school year, with the plan that I could return in 2008–2009.

After that, I limped through the final six months of the 2006–2007 school year, missing enough school to make me both question how I was able to keep my job, and to be ashamed of myself for not being able to show up for the kids. Sometimes I called in sick from sheer exhaustion, but I was also frequently ill. The constant pressure from my administrators, who were worried about the school's failing test scores, did not help. Of course I wanted these children to succeed, but my poor health dictated that I was past the point where I could come early, stay late, and spend hours of my own unpaid time making cheery bulletin boards.

Knowing it might well be my last year in the classroom, I rallied long enough to plan fun art projects and activities to do with my students after the state testing in May. But during the last week of school, I became terribly ill. A bout of non-stop vomiting landed me in the emergency room, and although the doctors performed a battery of tests, they couldn't find what was wrong with me. I was given anti-nausea medication that made me shake uncontrollably until I decided the continuous vomiting was preferable.

All in all, I ended up in the emergency room three times in three days, and no one ever figured out what was wrong. On the last day of school, I was so ill that a friend drove me to school to say goodbye to the kids and I was too weak to get out of the car or even to sit upright in the seat. The kids had to come to the car where I was lying down to say goodbye.

Not being able to finish the year with my students as planned or even getting to say a proper goodbye was heartbreaking. I'm not sure if they understood why I wasn't there that last week, which made me feel even worse, as they had already been abandoned by so many other people in their lives.

It took me three weeks to recover from that illness and the better part of the next year to recover my lost strength. Eventually, I started subbing a little during my year of leave (but not much, because the district kept losing my time sheet) and working as a copy editor and private tutor. Then one day in mid-February 2008, I woke up and thought, "I'm not tired anymore."

It had taken *eight months* for me to stop feeling exhausted.

It made me realize that I couldn't go back to the classroom—not unless something significant changed in the way things were run. I hated leaving the kids. That felt like giving up on them. But I knew going back would mean sliding back to my previous state of poor health, and I just couldn't do it.

A Safe Place to Land

Since I stopped teaching, I have much more energy.

I no longer avoid my friends due to feeling tired all the time. I don't get sick nearly as often—and I'm not just talking about colds and flus from children's germs. I have fewer tension headaches, too. When, occasionally, I wonder out loud about the possibility of going back into the classroom (I still miss it), my friends who were around during that time of my life get agitated and tell me not to, reminding me of the toll it took on my health.

But I'm one of the lucky ones. I eventually found a job where I could still help children without working for the broken public school system. Most of my friends who have left teaching ended up going into fields that don't involve working with children anymore, and many of them miss it. As difficult as it was—both professionally and personally—teaching the children of this particular community was incredibly rewarding.

For three years, I worked as the Director of Education at Harbor House, a Christian non-profit organization in Oakland. Except for the non-profit salary, it was basically my ideal job. I was able to spend my days creating a program that supported academic growth *and* told kids how much God loves them.

Even though Harbor House is a Christian organization, the kids who attend their programs come from Hindu, Muslim, Buddhist, Protestant, and Catholic homes, leading to a great mix of perspectives when they are engaged in conversation. Children attend who have roots in Cambodia, Nigeria, Tanzania, Mexico, Guatemala, China, Vietnam, Sri Lanka, Thailand, and more, along with African American and Native American students.

This incredible diversity is one of the greatest strengths of this organization; it promotes the kids' opportunities to learn to respect and coexist with others from different backgrounds. I also supervised the classroom leaders: young adults who mainly grew up in similar circumstances to the younger students. These young adults can reach the students in ways that I, personally, was not able to, and so they're role models the kids really look up to.

But what I loved most about this job, which I left to write this book, is that I was able to support the academic growth of our students without the public school district's idiosyncrasies, administrative chaos, and impossible expectations. I was still able to help the children learn, often in one-on-one or small group situations, but I didn't have to test them.

In this role, I could also take the time to help the students mature emotionally and interpersonally. I was honored to see incredible growth in many of the children and even in some of the parents; the support Harbor House staff provides the children helps parents tremendously.

Part of the reason why Harbor House works so well is its family structure. The staff cares for the whole child—so much so that the children very often regard staff members like older siblings. The children learn that everyone is a part of God's family, and that it doesn't matter what they look like, what language they speak, or where they're from— we humans are a family, and we look out for each other.

The View from Here

Now, nearly a decade after making the decision to leave the public school classroom, I have the distance and clarity to realize that I will probably not return to it. But it's important to me that "my kids," those from both East Oakland Elementary and Harbor House, thrive in their public education and beyond. My frontline teaching experience proved to me that a single classroom teacher could never make the changes that the system needs, and trying to do so is a sure recipe for overwork, ill health, and ultimate failure. If I can't change the system from within it, I'm equally skeptical of the prospects of reforming public education at the district, state, or national level based on current strategies.

Many of the current players are simply too steeped in the system to change. I hear principals talk about how teachers must not "waste one minute" of learning time, and I mourn for children's lost playtime. This is a vital component of a child's learning process, yet public education seems to have no room left for it. I hear stories from kids who dread testing and from teachers who feel like sadists for administering those same tests.

These stories echo the ones I lived through a decade ago, and the lack of progress makes it feel insurmountable to effect systemic change. I long for everyone—both those who work in education and those who don't—to recognize how important all children are and to act accordingly. I will continue to do what I can, extoling Harbor House as a model of a holistic environment for nurturing our youth, and seeking concerned parents and partners to reverse the trend of education inequality.

Our students aren't failing school. Our schools are failing the students.

By writing this book, I hope to start a conversation: first we need to face the harsh reality of education inequality in this country, and second, we need to come up with workable solutions that ensure all children truly have equal access and opportunity to better themselves and their lives—and, in turn, the lives of their own future generations—through education.

We need to work together—administrators, parents, teachers, and students—to create something closer to the Harbor House model: a place that nurtures students and their families by bringing people together as part of a larger family, one that is both caring and challenging, can show tough love and forgiveness, and always keeps the students' best interests closest at heart.

For those kids who are most vulnerable, this is nothing short of a matter of life and death.

EPILOGUE

Elijah: A Celebratory Graduation

For teachers in East Oakland, every student success story is cause for celebration, and success stories come in many different forms. We celebrate when our students graduate from elementary school and middle school. We cry for joy at high school graduations because we know how much the kids accomplished within an education system that sets them up for failure in almost every way.

My students were as smart as any other class of students—of any demographic or from any neighborhood. But for eight years as their teacher, and in the years since then, I've watched the cycle of poverty and violence they were born into take its terrible toll on their educational and future life prospects. College-educated role models and enriching educational opportunities are scarce for these kids, which often keeps them from pursuing higher education[11]. When I see former students who are gainfully and legally employed, who are raising children in a nurturing environment, or who are working their way through community college while trying to support their family, I count this as a resounding success.

One of my former third-grade students recently invited me to be his guest at his graduation from an independent study program that catered to students who didn't do well with the social aspects of high school. The ceremony was jointly held with a continuation school (an alternative way for students to earn a high school diploma when they are at risk for a variety of reasons).

It made me think back to my own high school graduation, an exciting time for me; I was a class speaker and award recipient, and I had a big

[11] http://time.com/3506103/income-college-attendance/. See also: https://www.dosomething.org/us/facts/11-facts-about-education-and-poverty-america

party. But this was expected. Not one person in my life doubted that I would graduate from high school.

In contrast, the kids at this graduation came from a different background. Many of them were not expected to graduate—or even make it to—high school. Various students in this graduating class had been addicted to drugs, kicked out of their homes, homeless, or in abusive relationships. Or they'd had babies, or had to take on other adult responsibilities that children should never have to shoulder.. (Too often we forget that yes, teenagers are still children.) Having persevered in the face of such challenges to get their education, these graduates had much to celebrate, and the ceremony had a distinctly party-like atmosphere.

The graduation wasn't very well organized and the adult speakers were either unprepared, nervous, or both. It was hot in the gym and the program was long and not closely followed. None of that mattered. The ceremony was wonderful because it represented so much accomplishment.

The student who had invited me to watch him walk the stage that day was Elijah, who went to Washington, DC in eighth grade and met President Obama. I wrote about him and his trip, and shared an essay of his in chapter 9, but in short, Elijah was a smart, hard-working child who faced all the issues that any young black man faces in Oakland and in the United States as a whole. Additionally, he and his family had survived a house fire in which they were physically unharmed but lost everything, forced to watch their house burn to the ground.

Later, as an early teen, Elijah was in a bad bicycle accident that landed him in the hospital. As he transitioned into a large high school, his performance and grades slipped a little (the accident and house fire probably contributing to lingering trauma). Unfortunately, his guidance counselor was completely overwhelmed and did what many high school guidance counselors have to do: deal with only the biggest problems, which meant ignoring students like Elijah who weren't causing problems for teachers or other students.

When the counselor's inattention caused Elijah to be mistakenly placed into classes he had already taken and passed, Elijah rebelled and responded by purposely failing the classes the second time around. He felt he shouldn't have to take them again, especially given that it seemed unlikely he would get additional credits toward graduation for repeating courses he'd already passed. It's hard to argue with that.

Lacking effective tools to advocate for himself when his designated advocate fell down on the job, Elijah fell too far behind his peers to catch up. Combined with an effort to escape "hanging out with bad influences" (his words), he made the very difficult and mature decision to switch to an independent study school and live with the stigma that he wouldn't graduate with his friends.

There were other students I recognized at that graduation, including another boy from one of my third-grade classes. In addition, a girl who was facing expulsion hearings back when I had been her substitute teacher was both a graduate and a speaker. I was flabbergasted and delighted that she had made it. I hadn't known her long, but recalled that she had been a particularly angry child. In my experience, angry students, especially students of color, were usually labeled by the district as "defiant" and directed to continuation schools—or they simply dropped out of school altogether. Another speaker gave her speech clutching a box of ashes—clearly a lost loved one, although I don't know whom.

We often define success as graduating from high school, going to college, graduating again, and getting a well-paying job. But in the case of kids who succeeded in spite of an educational system that seemed all but rigged against them, graduating from high school was an accomplishment that took hard work and perseverance. I was incredibly proud watching Elijah and my other former students walk across that stage.

Suzanne: The Power of Joy and Determination

While the students at Elijah's school were seen by many as unlikely to make it to graduation, I knew from the beginning of her third-grade year that Suzanne was going to thrive.

When Suzanne was a little girl, the first thing everyone noticed about her was her smile. Although she had lived in East Oakland her whole life and faced many of the same struggles and challenges as the other kids, she had the most joyful smile I've ever seen, and she wore it frequently.

This may seem a small thing, but such happiness was rare among my students, and it was the first sign I saw that assured me she was going to be all right.

Suzanne lived with her dad, and I could see from the start that her positive attitude was a testament to his loving support in her life. Later, I was able to get to know Suzanne's mother and even though the two parents were not together as a couple, I saw how they worked together for their daughter's success.

In middle and high school, Suzanne earned several opportunities to attend leadership forums. These were selective events, requiring a serious application process complete with letters of recommendation. But even acceptance left the challenge of paying for them, and they didn't come cheap. Suzanne attended events in Washington, DC, London, and Paris, and in contrast to most of the other students on those trips, who just had their parents write a check, Suzanne had to raise the funds herself. I contributed, as well as other teachers, friends of mine, her church community, and more. The confidence and persistence she gained by working to reach these goals, as well as the experiences of the events themselves, were transformational. I saw her grow from a generally happy girl—who could nonetheless be fairly reactive when someone baited her—into a strong, self-assured young woman who does not let the many obstacles she has faced stand in the way of her goals.

Suzanne graduated from high school and went on to attend Howard University, where—at the time of this writing—she is still a student. There she has continued to develop her leadership skills by becoming a resident advisor in her dorm and exploring medical mission trips in South Africa. She continues to be proud of where she comes from, her heritage, and who she is. I can't wait to see what Suzanne continues to accomplish as she finishes her undergraduate studies and continues to make her way in the world.

Rosa: First-Generation College Graduate

Rosa was my first (and to my knowledge, so far my only) student to graduate from college. Her parents immigrated to the United States from Mexico before she was born. Due to circumstances beyond their control, neither of her parents was able to complete their education— her mother dropped out after sixth grade, because she went to the States to work and help support her family. Her father didn't make it past kindergarten because his family could not afford shoes for him.

In part because of their own limited educational opportunities, Rosa's parents raised their daughter to value education. Even with her own elementary level education, Rosa's mother taught her child how to read and write in Spanish at home, making Rosa one of the few kids at our school who started kindergarten knowing how to read (in any language). So it was with particular pride, in the summer of 2015, that I watched as Rosa became the first person in her family to graduate from college. Ever.

Rosa lived very close to the school I taught at, in a neighborhood that is not safe now and was much worse when she was in elementary school. She has memories of lockdowns throughout all of her school years. Indeed, having a school day disrupted due to nearby gunfire was commonplace, hardly enough to faze her—though she admitted that her year in my stand-alone "portable" classroom, which lacked exterior doors that could be locked, made her feel more vulnerable. Like most of my students, Rosa grew to think of this level of violence as normal, right up until her senior year of high school. One day the sound of gunshots interrupted an SAT tutoring session, and one of the tutors (who was not from the neighborhood) started to cry. Initially confused, Rosa finally recognized how desensitized she had become to the violence that surrounded her.

Being a hard worker did not mean that school was always easy for her. Although she was the co-valedictorian of her high school class, with a 4.0 grade point average, Rosa was not adequately prepared for college because her high school lacked academic rigor. Her freshman year was rough enough that she came back home to attend community college and improve her study skills. Upon returning to UCLA, she was able to bring her GPA up.

Rosa had another awakening when she took a class in UCLA's Chicano Studies program and researched her home school district as part of a project. Compared to other districts, she found an abysmal lack of resources in Oakland and many other low-income areas, along with teachers who were much less qualified, such as first-year Teach For America[12] teachers and other new educators who lacked proper training or preparation. She also learned about how No Child Left Behind had hurt under-resourced schools the most, and how changes in education law in California took away many resources from kids who came into school not speaking English.

What she learned was shocking, and yet it made sense given Rosa's own educational experience growing up in East Oakland. Resources at her high school were few and far between. Many classes had no books at all, and her chemistry class lacked any lab equipment. The one experiment she remembers from her year of chemistry was burning Cheetos to see what happened to them. The abysmal science offerings meant that Rosa was effectively cut off from pursuing this field in college because she would have started so far behind her classmates. She had some wonderful teachers but says that many of the good ones were fired due to what she thinks were personal problems with the administration. Other teachers admitted that they "weren't used to the environment"— code for teaching low-income and minority students.

Her high school also made some administrative mistakes that set Rosa back. One snafu meant that Rosa had to take a required art course at a community college in her senior year instead of at her high school her junior year as she desired. The added stress her senior year (along with worrying about college applications and financial aid) resulted in migraines so severe that she required several hospital visits that year.

In addition, her school also mistakenly listed her GPA as 3.33 instead of 4.0 right around the time that she was applying to colleges. Only a threatened complaint to the district office resolved the situation—a mistake that could have kept her out of many colleges and disqualify her for untold grants and scholarships.

---

[12] Teach For America (TFA) is a well-meaning program that brings teachers into underserved communities to fill teacher shortages. That said, TFA recruits receive only five weeks of training and are placed in schools that often resemble East Oakland Elementary in demographics, problems, and lack of support. It's definitely a sink-or-swim model.

I was able to attend Rosa's UCLA graduation. It was the *La Raza* graduation, for Latino and Chicano students from all majors, and it was at times like a big party. Much of the program was in Spanish and it was very family-oriented—all the speakers touched on the importance of community and family. My favorite thing about it was that each graduate was introduced by name with the addition of *"hijo de . . . "* or *"hija de . . . "* [son or daughter of . . .] recognizing the triumph of the whole family in these achievements.

At the time of this writing, Rosa is currently working at her old high school and saving up money to begin the application process for law school. She has no road map for this; she's never seen what happens after you get a college degree. And it will be hard for her to leave her family again for law school. But she's determined to achieve her dream of starting a community center in Oakland that can offer services to undocumented residents and youth at risk of incarceration or gang violence, as well as rehabilitation and job resources for ex-felons. I have every confidence the work she is so passionate about will make a crucial difference in countless lives.

Believe It, So We Can Change It

When I say that educational inequality is a matter of life and death for kids like my former students, I'm not exaggerating. Many of the students I taught did not expect to survive past the age of twenty-five. As I've said, most did not expect to go to college, and even graduating from high school was not a given for many of them. A wide variety of professionals, from psychologists to leadership experts, have observed that most people tend to internalize and live either up or down to the expectations that other people—particularly loved ones, role models, and authority figures—place on them.

I have seen this to be true. When kids are told from the beginning of their educational career that they are "slow" or "bad," or given the message—explicitly or implicitly—that they're undervalued or unlikely to succeed, they quickly grow to believe it. Worse, for people in communities like East Oakland, these kinds of ideas can be internalized by entire families and passed down to future generations, making such negative assumptions about one's self worth that much harder to overcome. Given the inequities they face, these students already have to work much harder than their more privileged counterparts to get to the same place. And many must engage in this struggle while bearing up under the additional weight of having to prove these negative expectations about themselves wrong—to both themselves and the world at large.

In addition, such inequities have existed for so long that even students who do succeed academically in communities like East Oakland struggle to find role models to help guide their way forward in life. Many of my students had to start working at a young age or take on other extensive family obligations, and thus were unable to focus on school. Others did well academically but had no idea which classes to take to prepare for higher education, or how to apply for college or financial aid. Some of them ended up going to college only to drop out in their first year because they didn't know how to navigate higher education and didn't know anyone who could help them.

We like to say that we have come a long way, and in some ways this is true. Legal segregation does not exist anymore, and yes, we have had a black president. However, real progress for the average child of color growing up in a place like East Oakland has been excruciatingly slow. And the children I taught deserved better than they got.

"Literally unbelievable." To this day, this common reaction from family and friends when I tell them stories from my teaching days rings in my ears.

Well, believe it. And once you've seen the heartbreaking truth of how we're failing these kids, don't turn away from it. Please. The first step in achieving the change we need is accepting the truth of the education inequity that is present now, today.

But the question remains for each of us—parents, students, educators, administrators, policy makers, and concerned citizens alike. What will we do about it?

ACKNOWLEDGMENTS

This book would not have been possible without my incredible, wonderful students. I am so thankful for my class of first graders and my seven classes of third graders, along with all the other students who weren't in my class but felt like part of the family anyway. You all brought joy and purpose to my life, even when our time together was tinged with great sadness. I continue to wish I could have done more. My thanks go out also to all of the families who shared their children with me, not just at school but at birthday parties, T-ball games, and family gatherings. There are more wonderful parents than I can list, but thank you to Catrina Gray, who hunted me down to tell me her baby was graduating from high school, and to Charlene Johnson and Lesli Reed, who found me on Facebook and keep me updated on their precious kids (now adults). James Buggs, you raised a wonderful daughter and we all miss you greatly. It was an incredible honor to be invited to Roxana Hurtado's graduation from UCLA and to attend Stephanie Buggs's and Saafir Birchett's high school graduations.

Teaching in Oakland was tough. There were some staff at my school who made everything harder and others who helped me survive. Michelle Hinck, Daphne Ocampo, and Stephanie Kondrashoff, thank you for welcoming me as a brand new, shell-shocked teacher and helping me through many, many problems. Later, I was honored to work with or near, among others: Alene Hearing, Marjorie Bellande, Nikita Gibbs, Patrice Simmons, Jen Sethasang, Sara White Green, Emily Penner, Dennis Guikema, Elizabeth Willard, Seema Saluja, Barbara Karvelot, Pak Khuth, Bruce Ridgeway, and Cheryl Wilson. You all left your mark on me during that time, and you are all still making a difference. None of us had an easy time at "East Oakland Elementary" but I'm so proud of how we touched lives.

Thanks to Lindsay LaShell for being the first to tell me that these stories were "literally unbelievable," and that I needed to write them down. Thanks to Jessica Margolin for steadfastly encouraging me to keep blogging and eventually sitting down with me to actually start the book process by literally cutting and pasting. To Debbie Rogers, an outstanding teacher, thank you for serving as my resource for understanding special education hurdles and definitions during the writing process.

I volunteered at Westminster Woods (a Presbyterian camp in Sonoma County, California) in high school and worked there during my college years. It was there that I learned I love working with children, promoting mutual respect, and appreciating each child's personality and unique gifts. There are too many people at Westminster Woods to thank each of you individually, but I'm eternally grateful for that experience, which has greatly shaped my professional life and work.

Thank you to the children of the YMCA in Sacramento. You taught me to love under-resourced children and not be afraid of them.

My dear friends who run the orphanage Pilar de Esperanza in Reynosa, Mexico reminded me over and over through teaching and writing that I could trust God. I needed that reminder more times than I can count.

Many people have helped me spread the word about the book, and I've learned the most from Lindsay LaShell, Bronwyn Emery, Steve Ketchpel, and Jonathan Henke. Lindsay LaShell and Jonathan Henke were also extremely patient in providing technical help and created everything on my website except the words.

I owe a debt of gratitude to the staff, families, and children of Harbor House for understanding when I needed to leave to finish this project and for carrying on the amazing work happening there.

Members of my writing group, To Live and Write in Alameda, encouraged me, helped me find "Jorge" in prison, and gave me tips for telling people about the book. A special thank you to Bronwyn Emery for starting the group and making it a welcoming and supportive place. I found this writing group after I had already written most of a book, but they helped me learn and embrace that I was a writer, and I will forever be grateful.

Thank you to my editor, Julia Watson, who helped me take a rough manuscript still mostly in blog form and make it into a real book. I didn't even remotely understand what I was trying to do at times, and she did. Steve Ketchpel, Natalie Conrow, and Jessica Margolin all did substantial editing at various points in the process. Steve Ketchpel helped me understand that I could self-publish a book and walked me through the whole process in great detail. Christine Osborne provided excellent copyediting on a very timely basis.

Thank you to Merrilee Willoughby for the beautiful head shot on a day I was feeling less than beautiful. Thank you to Damian Ludwig for providing the wonderful graphic art for the cover, promotional materials, and social media, and for accommodating my needs with grace and patience. Even the most critical people I know loved the cover art. Thank you to Marites D. Bautista for the beautiful layout and the extremely fast turnaround. Miguel Lopez made my book his capstone project for his Digital Marketing Certificate, with the generous support of his employer, Diamond + Branch Marketing Group, and used his knowledge of social media and digital marketing to help me greatly.

Thank you to my family. The fact that every member of my immediate family came to visit my classroom, even when doing so fell pretty far out of everyone's comfort zone, showed their willingness to learn and to support me. I have an incredibly supportive group of friends who help me survive everything thrown my way; without them, this book would never have been written.

Thank you.

APPENDIX

The challenges I encountered while I taught in Oakland and have explored throughout this book are fraught with complicated issues on all sides. For those readers who wish to learn more about these issues—either to get involved themselves or simply to become better educated about them—I've included information about some recommended references to serve as a starting point.

The following list is by no means comprehensive, but these are resources that either helped me along the way or that I particularly admire.

Books

While all of Jonathan Kozol's books are well worth reading and shed light on inequality in schools, *Savage Inequalities: Children in America's Schools* is the one that opened the eyes of many to just how blatant the gap is between the rich and the poor—even in public schools. *The Shame of the Nation: The Restoration of Apartheid Schooling in America* is another of Kozol's books that explains how we are returning to a segregated America in public education, and how prison tactics are often used in inner-city schools

The New Jim Crow: Mass Incarceration in the Age of Colorblindness by Michelle Alexander is a powerful exposition of how people of color are still discriminated against despite the fact that legal segregation is supposedly over. Even with everything I know about how law and prison systems can still affect African Americans and other minorities, I was shocked at how entrenched this is in our legal and corrections system.

There are many, many books about the detrimental effects of standardized testing in education. One of them is *The Case against Standardized*

Testing: Raising the Scores, Ruining the Schools by Alfie Kohn. Kohn explains how little test scores actually tell us, including the statistical problems with testing. He also discusses how the focus on high-stakes testing comes at the expense of other, more important and lasting, forms of learning.

The Explosive Child: A New Approach for Understanding and Parenting Easily Frustrated, Chronically Inflexible Children by Ross W. Greene is often recommended to parents, but teachers can benefit from this wisdom as well. The author explores inflexibility and explosiveness in children and what factors can bring out these behaviors. His interventions can help parents and teachers manage these children well and provide tools for them that reduce frustration.

Geoffrey Canada is best known for founding the Harlem Children's Zone. Before that, he was a black boy and young man growing up in the South Bronx. His memoir *Fist, Stick, Knife, Gun: A Personal History of Violence* shows how completely violence interacted with every part of his life and how the boys in the neighborhood were ranked through the rituals of fist, stick, and knife, eventually moving on to guns. This is similar to how many of my students grew up in Oakland.

I wish I had had a copy of *For White People Who Teach in the Hood… and the Rest of Y'all Too: Reality Pedagogy and Urban Education* by Christopher Emdin before I started teaching, but since he's only just published it, I'll try to get others to read before they teach! The author draws on his own experiences feeling marginalized in school as a young person of color and provides stories and pedagogy so that other teachers won't make the mistakes of his teachers.

For my students, murder was often a fact of life, and teaching a community that was traumatized was something I had to learn. *Ghettoside: A True Story of Murder in America* by Jill Leovy explores "ghettoside" murders that are often ignored. I can't count the amount of times that I knew of people who were murdered and essentially no investigation launched because the victim was just another dead black man in the ghetto.

Many people read a book like this and don't know what to do with the problems that were brought up. *Giving Back: Discover your values and put them into action through volunteering and donating,* by Dr. Steven Ketchpel, is a practical handbook on how to choose volunteer and donation opportunities that align with your values and interests. Complete with case studies and family activities, it is an excellent, hands-on resource for anyone who wants to cultivate gratitude for what they have and help those who are less privileged.

Every teacher has had students who were "defiant," a label far more often applied to black boys than any other student population. In *I Won't Learn from You: And Other Thoughts on Creative Maladjustment,* Herbert R. Kohl discusses how some students' "behavior problems" might be a way of standing up for themselves and practicing a "right to refuse." This should be read by every teacher.

Other People's Children: Cultural Conflict in the Classroom, by Lisa Delpit, is often required reading in teacher preparation programs, for good reason. Many of us white teachers walk into majority-minority schools with little or no understanding of any culture other than the dominant one—ours. Misunderstandings, prejudice, and miscommunication with students from other cultures or subcultures can cause significant damage even with the best intentions of the teacher. Delpit's other books are also well worth reading.

From another former Oakland teacher, Anthony Cody, *The Educator and the Oligarch: A Teacher Challenges the Gates Foundation* takes on the Gates Foundation and brings up all the problems with Gates (or any other private individual) essentially buying our public schools. Cody opposes the extreme focus on test prep and sheds light on other dangers from people who seem to help and are changing the face of public education, and not always for the better.

There Are No Children Here: The Story of Two Boys Growing Up in the Other America by Alex Kotlowitz is one of the first books that opened my eyes to what it is like to live in the kind of violence I didn't think existed in the United States. Kotlowitz tells the story of two boys living in a Chicago housing project famous for poverty, violence, and drugs. The title was what made the book so haunting for me. When asked about her children, the mother being interviewed said, "But you know, there are no children here. They've seen too much to be children." That quote stayed with me all through my teaching career as I saw it over and over.

Documentaries

Although I have not been able to watch it because it hits too close to home, *Fruitvale Station,* directed by Ryan Coogler, tells the story of how one black man in Oakland was killed by a transit police officer. I did see the protests and riots in the aftermath of both the shooting and the sentencing of the officer (he was convicted of involuntary manslaughter and spent less than a year in jail). This film is not a documentary, but a feature film based on true events. The tragic incident has greatly shaped community-police relations in Oakland and shows the great divide that continues to plague conversations about race, police violence, and much more.

The Interrupters, a film by Steve James and Alex Kotlowitz, is a powerful documentary about CeaseFire, part of the Chicago Project for Violence Prevention. Violence Interrupters, including the daughter of a famed former Chicago gang leader, literally interrupt street violence. It is terrifying and inspirational and discouraging all at once, and I highly recommend it.

Tavis Smiley's documentary *Too Important to Fail* takes a good look at the unique challenges faced by teenage African American boys. Smiley respectfully listens to and follows the young men when they explain what went wrong and what would have been different. "Fred" in my book was featured in this documentary.

Websites and Podcasts

Oakland Unified School District Data, found at www.ousddata.org, provides an overview of current conditions in OUSD although it does not go back to the years I was teaching. However, if you enjoy data and want to see what is going on in my former district, this website has a plethora of data for you.

Malcolm Gladwell dedicates three episodes of his podcast *Revisionist History* to inequity in higher education. The episodes "Carlos Doesn't Remember," "Food Fight," and "My Little Hundred Millions" consider how unlikely it is for talented children living in poverty to go to college and succeed, and tackles inequity in higher education. (www.revisionisthistory.com)

The Stanford Center on Poverty & Inequality, at http://inequality. stanford.edu, has more podcasts, facts, figures, and explanations on poverty and inequality in the United States and how this affects children and families than I could ever possibly cite.

Teaching Tolerance: A Project of the Southern Poverty Law Center is a magazine as well as a network of extensive online resources including professional development, classroom materials, webinars, and more, all with the theme of respecting and valuing human diversity. I blogged for them for a while (www.tolerance.org/author/bronwyn-harris) and used their materials in my classroom when I was teaching.

I always enjoy *This American Life's* podcast, but every once in a while they have a series that I feel everyone should listen to. Episodes #562 and 563, "The Problem We All Live With," is one of those series. These episodes discuss school reforms and integration, and how they have both succeeded and failed in fighting educational inequity. (www.thisamericanlife.org)

People Who Are Helping

Worldwide:

Big Brothers Big Sisters (BBBS)
www.bbbs.org

What they do: Big Brothers Big Sisters performs very careful matches of a "Big" (adult) with a "Little" (child) of the same gender. Their staff provides ongoing support to the Big and to the Little's parents for the life of the match. My Little Sister and I have been matched for seven years, and it has been life-changing for both of us.

How you can get involved: Visit their website to find out how you can volunteer or donate.

Bikers Against Child Abuse International (BACA)
www.bacaworld.org

What they do: Bikers Against Child Abuse International is a non-profit organization made up of bikers (motorcyclists) whose goal is to "create a safer environment for abused children." The bikers, who have all had extensive background checks, work with local and state agencies to provide physical and emotional support for children who have been abused.

How you can get involved: Bikers around the world can go to their website to find out more about becoming involved, and all of us can donate.

Court-Appointed Special Advocates (CASA)
www.casaforchildren.org

What they do: Volunteers go through a careful screening process and are appointed by judges to advocate for neglected and abused children, providing a constant safe adult presence for children going through the court system. CASA volunteers are charged with spending time with the children and representing their best interest to the judge in charge of their case. Volunteering is a significant time commitment but extremely rewarding.

How you can get involved: CASA's website offers volunteer opportunities as well as ways to help financially.

DonorsChoose

www.donorschoose.org

What they do: DonorsChoose was started by a high school teacher in the Bronx in 2000, and it has now expanded nationwide and been publicized by comedian Stephen Colbert, who once granted all requests in his home state of South Carolina. Teachers can post any request for supplies for their classroom, in any subject, and donors can choose what they'd like to fund. I was extremely fortunate to be one of the pilot teachers in the Bay Area and had generous private donors fund everything from an abacus set to class pets to playground equipment for my classroom, saving me hundreds if not thousands of dollars out of my own pocket. Donors also get thank you notes from the kids, which is a wonderful personal touch.

How you can get involved: Find a project that you are interested in and fund all or part of it!

In the San Francisco Bay Area:

826 Valencia

www.826valencia.org

What they do: 826 Valencia is a non-profit founded by author Dave Eggers that equips and inspires teachers and students alike to write and love writing. They provide field trips, workshops, and college and career readiness programs for under-resourced students in San Francisco. 826 Valencia has expanded and now has seven other 826 branches across the United States.

How you can get involved: Visit their website to find out how you can volunteer or donate, or visit the pirate supply store at the front of the business to support them by buying pirate swag!

Faith Network of the East Bay
www.faith-network.com

What they do: Faith Network was founded in 2001 by an Oakland pastor who saw how much support was needed by under-resourced public schools and the staff at those schools. Faith Network's mission is to give hope to disadvantaged students in East Bay schools by surrounding them with a caring community, igniting their innate potential, and helping them to develop academic and life skills crucial to their growth and fulfillment. The goal is to prepare today's youth for a life of serving others and contributing positively to their communities. Faith Network has added a variety of programs in recent years, including CareerBridge, Science Horizons, and Health4Kids.

How you can get involved: If you are local to the San Francisco Bay Area, you can volunteer, and they are grateful for donations.

Harbor House Ministries
www.hhministries.org

What they do: Harbor House is a Christian non-profit that serves everyone in the Oakland community. They strive for a holistic approach: providing educational, spiritual, and economic programs. I ran the after-school and summer programs for three years and was honored to be able to teach the kids how much God loved them as well as helping them academically and supporting their parents in navigating the school system. Harbor House also provides ESL classes for adults, food distribution, a very low-cost Christmas store, and more.

How you can get involved: Harbor House takes volunteers and work groups at specific times and welcomes your financial donation, which helps pay for staff and programs for extremely under-resourced kids.

The Oakland Literacy Coalition
www.oaklandliteracycoalition.org

What they do: The Oakland Literacy Coalition is a non-profit that exists to meet the literacy needs of Oakland, particularly for the youngest readers, by improving the capacity and increasing the impact of Oakland's literacy providers. The Coalition fulfills this mission by providing opportunities for Oakland's literacy providers to learn, collaborate, and champion literacy in the community. The Coalition spearheads the Oakland Reads campaign aimed at dramatically increasing third grade reading achievement so that every Oakland child has the foundational literacy skills necessary to succeed in school and thrive. (OLC is largely run and funded by the Rogers Family Foundation, which supports charter schools in Oakland. While there are pros and cons to the charter school movement, I have been very happy with the OLC and my involvement with them.)

How you can get involved: Make a donation through the website, or learn how you can become a literacy volunteer with one of their member organizations.

The Oakland Public Education Fund

www.oaklandedfund.org

What they do: The Oakland Public Education Fund raises money for all public schools in Oakland, both traditional and charter, with a focus on the most under-resourced schools. They also build community relationships with organizations such as Running for a Better Oakland, Pandora (which sends employees to read in the schools), and local sports teams (that send players to visiting classrooms). Some critics point out that funneling donations through the Ed Fund can mean that the donations may receive less public scrutiny than otherwise, but overall, the OUSD employees I respect tend to be supportive of this group.

How you can get involved: The Oakland Public Education Fund accepts donations, either to their general fund or to a specific school, and welcomes volunteers.